Plant and Animal Ways

by

ILLA PODENDORF

ANNE NEIGOFF, *Managing Editor*

STANDARD EDUCATIONAL CORPORATION   *Chicago 1984*

Library of Congress Cataloging in Publication Data
Podendorf, Illa.
  Plant and animal ways.

  (Child horizons)
  Includes index.
  SUMMARY: Discusses the characteristics of a
representative sample from the world's wide variety
of animals and plants.
  1. Animals—Juvenile literature. 2. Plants—
Juvenile literature. [1. Animals. 2. Plants]
I. Title
QL49.P7   1978   574   78–4093
ISBN 0-87392–104-6

IT IS SEPTEMBER, and in the sky flocks of birds are winging southward. When winter is over and spring returns, the birds will come flying back again to their northern homes.

Birds do not have calendars to warn them of the approaching winter. They do not have maps or instruments to guide them. Yet they know when to fly south and how to get there. That is one of the wonders of nature.

Nature has many wonders. As we watch a beaver build its dam or ants scurrying in an anthill or a spider weaving its lacy web, we marvel at their knowledge and skill. The ways of the fish in the sea are marvelous, too. The Chinook, or king salmon, swims from far out in the Pacific Ocean to the Columbia River to lay its eggs. It is a long, long journey and a dangerous journey and yet each year thousands of salmon travel it.

The plant kingdom is full of wonders, too. There are plants so tiny that they can be seen only under a microscope. There are huge plants like the California sequoia and redwood trees that tower more than 300 feet tall. Some of the giant sequoias are more than 3,000 years old! They were ancient trees when Columbus discovered America. They are among the oldest known living things.

In this book, you will find stories about these plants and animals and many others. And as you read, you will discover, too, how all plants and animals depend upon each other to survive.

Did you ever think how we depend upon plants and animals? When men hunted and fished for their food and cut down trees to build log houses, they knew that without plants and animals they could not survive. Today we still depend upon plants and animals for much of our food and shelter.

Plants and animals give us other wonderful things. Can you imagine a world without the beauty and fragrance of flowers and the song of birds? Can you imagine a world without frisky puppies and kittens? The next time you go into your backyard or walk through a wood, see how many wonders of nature you can find!

Table of Contents

The Parade of Plants

WE ARE ALL LIVING THINGS

The Parade of Living Things

W HEN SOMEONE mentions a parade, you may think of people in uniform marching in step with lively band music. You may think of a long line of gaily decorated floats with people in colorful costumes. Or you may think of an exciting circus parade.

Those parades are fun, but the largest and most wonderful and most interesting parade is going on all the time all over the world. Every day it goes on right before your eyes even though you do not think of it as a parade. It is a *Parade of Living Things*.

Such a parade consists not only of animals. It includes plants too. Every living thing has a place in this parade. But to know what belongs in it we must know what things are alive.

7

What Is a Living Thing?

A PUPPY frisking in the snow-drift is alive. A baby robin in a nest and a little plant in a flowerpot are also alive. The puppy and the robin and the plant are different in many ways. In what ways are they all alike?

Like all living things, they grow.

The puppy grows into a dog. The baby robin grows up and flies away to build a nest of its own. The little plant may grow too big for its pot.

The snowdrift is not a living thing. It may get bigger as more and more snow falls on it, but it cannot grow by itself. The nest and the flowerpot cannot grow. They are not living things.

All livings things are alike in other ways, too. They all need food to grow. They also need air and water.

There is another important way in which living things are different from non-living things.

A puppy may grow up and have puppies of its own. A robin's egg hatches into a baby robin. A plant has seeds from which new plants may grow. But a nest cannot make a new nest. Living things, however, can produce more like themselves.

How many living things do you see in these pictures? How many non-living things? How do you know which are living things?

Plant or Animal?

THERE are many kinds of living things, but every living thing is either a plant or an animal.

Usually it is easy to tell if a living thing is a plant or an animal. Most animals can move. They get their food by eating plants and other animals.

Most plants cannot move. Green plants make their own food from substances in soil and water and from gases in the air.

But some plants and animals are so much alike that it is hard to know which they are.

Not all animals can move. Some ocean animals seem like plants because they fasten themselves to the ocean bottom as if they had roots.

Some plants are not green and cannot make their own food.

Some living things are so small that they can be seen only through a microscope. Yeast that makes bread rise and bacteria that cause food to spoil are plants like these. The amoeba, so tiny that thousands can live in a drop of water, is an animal like this.

Other living things are so very small and simple that scientists have not been able to tell whether they are plants or animals.

How many animals do you see? Do they all move in the same way? How many plants do you see?

9

Amoeba
(greatly magnified)

An amoeba is so tiny it can be seen only under a microscope. An animal can be as tiny as an amoeba or as huge as a whale.

Animals—Vertebrates and Invertebrates

THE parade of plants and animals has been going on millions of years but scientists are still learning new things about them. Later on in this book you will find more about the plant parade, but now let's find out more about animals.

There are many different kinds of animals, but scientists divide all animals into two main groups.

In one group are the animals with backbones. A backbone is made up of little bones fitted together like queerly shaped beads on a string. These little bones are called *vertebrae* so animals that have backbones are called *vertebrates*.

In the other group are all the animals that do not have backbones. These are called *invertebrates*.

You have a backbone, so you are a vertebrate. Horses, dogs, birds, fishes, toads, and snakes are other common vertebrates. Some invertebrate animals we see often are moths, butterflies, spiders, crayfish, and snails. As you will notice, vertebrate animals are usually larger than invertebrates. Can you think of a reason why?

A vertebrate animal has a

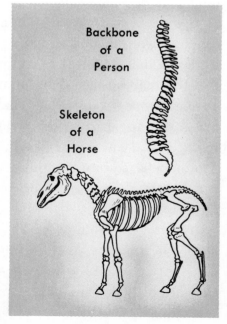

Backbone
of a
Person

Skeleton
of a
Horse

You and a horse both have backbones. You both have skeletons, but they are shaped in different ways.

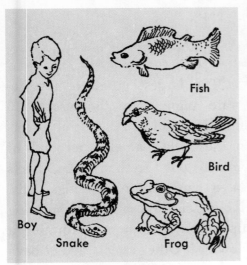

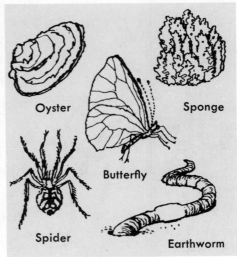

Vertebrates
(Animals with Backbones)

Invertebrates
(Animals without Backbones)

skeleton. The skeleton is made up of all the bones in an animal's body. The way the skeleton is fitted together gives the body its shape. A fish has a different shape from that of a bird because its skeleton is shaped differently.

The skeleton helps to protect the delicate organs on the inside of the body, such as the heart and the brain. Like the beams and girders of a skyscraper, the bones of the skeleton support the body and all its parts.

The skeleton helps the body move, too. A jointed skeleton helps animals to walk, swim, fly, and crawl.

Invertebrate animals have no skeletons to support their bodies. Some invertebrates have no hard parts. A few, such as the amoeba, have no definite shape.

Some invertebrate animals, such as sponges and barnacles, are not able to move about when adults. When young, they fasten themselves to something and remain there for life. Barnacles, for example, often fasten themselves to ship hulls.

Some invertebrate animals have hard outer coverings that help them to move, protect themselves, and keep their shapes. Do you wonder why the hard, outer covering does not keep these animals from growing? If the covering of a crayfish gets too small, the crayfish splits it open, crawls out of it, and a new covering forms on its body. Snails and oysters add new rims to their shells and in this way make their shells larger.

11

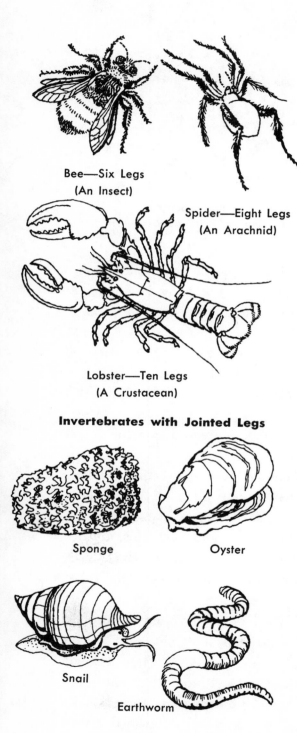

Bee—Six Legs
(An Insect)

Spider—Eight Legs
(An Arachnid)

Lobster—Ten Legs
(A Crustacean)

Invertebrates with Jointed Legs

Sponge

Oyster

Snail

Earthworm

The largest group of invertebrate animals are the insects. In fact there are more kinds of insects in the world than all other kinds of animals put together. Some insects have hard, outer coverings. Like the crayfish, they grow by splitting open this covering and forming a new one. Other insects do not have this protective hard cover. Measuring worms, green tomato worms, and little white grubs are insects like these.

There are many different kinds of insects, but there is one way in which all insects are alike.

Every insect has six legs. When you see an animal with six legs, you can be sure it is an insect. Even the caterpillar, which will some day be an adult insect, has six true legs.

Another group of invertebrate animals have eight legs. The spider belongs to this group.

Lobsters, crayfish, and crabs have ten legs.

Oysters have no legs at all. They have two shells, and they belong to still another group.

There are so many kinds of animals that you may never learn all their names. But if you find the common likeness of a group, you will be able to tell to which group an animal belongs.

Other Invertebrates

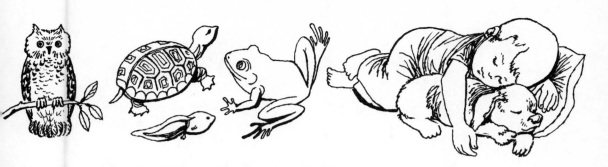

Where Do These Animals Belong?

HOW does a scientist find out about animals? He observes and asks questions. What kind of body does an animal have? Does it have fur or a scaly skin? How does it move? What food does it eat? Are its babies born or do they come from an egg? What other animals look and live in this way? When the scientist finds the answers, he knows in which group an animal belongs. Scientists divide all the vertebrates, or animals with backbones, into five groups.

If an animal has hair or fur anywhere on its body and if it feeds its babies milk from milk glands, it is a mammal. There is another way most mammals are alike. Most mammal babies are born.

If an animal has feathers, it is a bird. You may think of feathers as little signs that say "I am a bird." Baby birds come from eggs.

Reptiles are like birds and mammals in one way. They breathe with lungs. But most reptiles have scales on the outside of their bodies.

Most fishes have scales, too, but they have gills in place of lungs. Their gills take air out of the water. Watch a goldfish open and close its mouth. The water goes into the mouth and over the gills and from under the gill covers on the sides of its head.

Baby amphibians are like fishes in a way. When they first hatch they live in water and breathe with gills. But as amphibians grow older, they develop lungs and most of them, therefore, are able to come out on land. Then they are more like reptiles.

Mammals and birds are alike in an important way. They are *warm-blooded*. Their temperatures stay almost the same all the time. For example, your temperature is usually about 98.6° unless you are ill. Even then it never goes many degrees higher or lower. The temperature of birds is higher than ours, as high as 112°.

All other vertebrate animals—reptiles, amphibians, fishes—are *cold-blooded*. Their temperatures change to follow closely that of the air or water in which they live.

A Parade
Millions of Years Old

WHEN did the Parade of Living Things begin? Scientists believe the first living things appeared on earth about a billion years ago. Animal life began with a very simple creature like the amoeba. Then gradually more complex invertebrates developed. Then probably came the fishes, the amphibians, reptiles, birds, and finally the mammals.

How do scientists know? They have pieced together the story from a careful study of rocks. As millions of years passed, layer after layer of new rock was formed. Preserved in each layer were traces of life that had existed on earth at that time.

After the first vertebrates appeared, there were so many fishes that that period of time is called the Age of Fishes. Later great swamp forests covered much of the world. During this time so many kinds of amphibians developed that the period is often called the Age of Amphibians. Then came the Age of Reptiles and then the Age of Mammals. Man is the most intelligent mammal.

Man changed many things in the life around him to fit his needs. We live in the Age of Man.

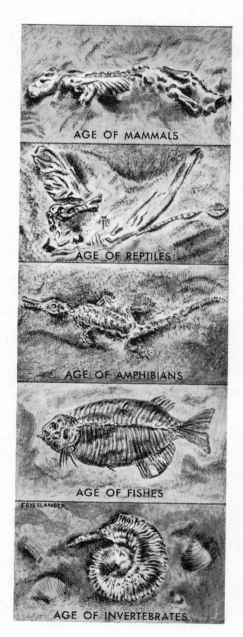

These drawings show impressions in rock of animals that lived many, many years ago. The impressions are called fossils. The pictures on the opposite page show some typical animals from these five Ages.

Brontotherium
This mammal was
15 feet long and
8 feet high.

Tyrannosaurus rex
The dinosaur, or terrible
lizard, is the best known
ancient reptile. This
dinosaur was probably
the fiercest animal that
ever stalked the earth.

Eryops
This early amphibian
looked like a huge
tadpole.

Dinichthys
This giant
early fish
had a huge
armored head.

Trilobite
This was one of the earliest invertebrate
animals. It lived in the sea and had more
than 20 legs on each side of its body. It had
a horny shell and breathed through gills.

MAMMALS

Man's Faithful Friend, the Dog

FOR many thousands of years, dogs have been companions for people. Even long ago when our ancestors lived in caves, they had their dogs, for the dog was one of the first animals tamed by man. Some other animals may be more important to us—cows because they give us milk and other food, sheep because they furnish us with food and wool for clothing—but as man's friend, the dog comes first.

Like his wild relatives, the wolf, the coyote, and the jackal, the dog has the sharp, pointed teeth of a *carnivorous,* or meat-eating, mammal. He is like his wild cousins in other ways, too. Before the dog was tamed, he, too, lived and hunted in groups called *packs.*

Dogs have eyes that are quick to see the flutter of a leaf or other motion. But a dog cannot see red, green, or other colors. All things look black, white, or gray to him. But he can hear sounds we cannot hear, and he has an especially good nose with which he can smell the faintest odor. These help make the dog a good hunter. Even today if we do not feed a dog, he can hunt and catch his own food.

Did you ever notice a dog's feet? He has five toes on his front paws and four toes on his hind paws. Each toe has a sharp claw on it, but the claws are not strong enough for climbing trees.

A dog is an intelligent animal, devoted and loyal to its master. Sometimes a child may quarrel with his human playmates and they will go away and leave him alone. But his dog will stay with him and lick his hands as if to say, "Here I am. I still like you."

Sometimes a boy may become angry or impatient with his dog. The dog will go off to lie down but soon will be back wagging its tail as if to say, "Please do not be angry with me."

Because the dog is faithful and loyal, some dogs are trained to act as guide dogs and lead their blind masters from place to place and to keep them out of danger. These dog guides are usually German Shepherds although Boxers, Labrador Retrievers, and certain other breeds are sometimes used.

A dog guide wears a harness with a stiff leash. His master directs him by saying "Left" or "Right." The dog signals his master through the harness when there are steps or other obstacles in the way.

A dog guide is taught to disobey as well as to obey. If his master asks to go across a street busy with traffic, the dog will not obey until it is safe to cross. It takes about four months to train a dog guide to help the blind.

Seeing Eye Dog, Inc.

The first dog guides in the United States were called Seeing Eye dogs because they were trained at Seeing Eye, Inc. of Morristown, New Jersey. Today there are about ten schools for dog guides in our country.

17

Collie

Newfoundland

Boxer

Great Dane

Eskimo

St. Bernard

Bloodhound

These dogs work for man.

Dogs help men in many other ways. Shepherds, collies, and many other breeds make good farm dogs and help the farmer tend his sheep, hogs, and cattle.

Some dogs are trained to help a small boy keep a herd of sheep together in a pasture. Other dogs learn to go out alone in fields or woods to find the cows, round them up, and take them to the barn so they will be there when the farmer is ready to milk them.

When pigs or cows get into a garden, farm dogs will nip at their heels just enough to send them hurrying back where they belong.

How would you like a sled ride behind a team of husky Eskimo dogs? People in snowy lands of the far north depend on these dogs for much of their transportation.

Many dogs are good watch dogs, too, and will not allow strangers to come near a child or house they are guarding. Other dogs, such as bloodhounds, are trained to help policemen find missing people.

These are hunting dogs.

Pointer

Cocker Spaniel

Irish Setter

English Setter

Beagle

Irish Water Spaniel

Dogs have been helping men for thousands and thousands of years. The cave man trained his dog to hunt with him. Today dogs still help men hunt. They sniff the air and almost like magic catch the scent of a covey of quail several yards away or pick up the trail of a rabbit. During a fox hunt, dogs lead the chase and locate the fox for the hunters.

Some dogs are trained to stay close to the hunter. When a hunter shoots a duck or pheasant, the dog watches carefully to see where the bird falls. Then, at a signal from its master, it will race away to get the bird. Most dogs, even dainty little pets, show some hunting spirit.

The dog works with man, hunts with man, and is man's friend.

These toy dogs and terriers are friendly pets.

Pomeranian

Pekinese

Scottish Terrier

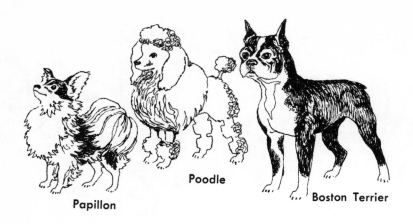

Poodle

Papillon

Boston Terrier

Even in time of war, dogs help men. Many dogs serve bravely on the battlefields, dashing through enemy fire to carry messages that are fastened to their collars. Others are trained to find wounded men and take help to them. War dogs walk guard duty. They carry packs of medical supplies and telephone wires even while the great guns boom. The use of dogs in warfare is not new. Dogs have fought beside men since the day of the cave man.

What kind of dog do you have? Is it a Great Dane or a tiny toy poodle? Is it a hunting dog or a champion show dog? Every year there are hundreds of dog shows in the United States and other countries. Judges examine each show dog carefully to decide whether it is the best of its breed. How proud the dog's master is when it wins the blue ribbon for Best of Show!

In other contests called *field trials*, dogs are judged for their skill as hunting dogs. In *obedience trials*, dogs are judged in another way. How good are their dog manners? Do they *sit*, *stay*, and *heel* the instant their masters command?

Not all dogs can win blue ribbons. But if you have a dog, you know that to you it is a champion. And to any dog, no matter what size or color, its own master is the most important person in the world!

20

Fox Terrier

The papillon,
the poodle,
the Boston Terrier,
and the fox terrier
make good pets, too.

The black squirrel makes his home in forests and orchards from Canada to Florida and as far west as Minnesota.

The Frisky Squirrel

A FLASH of bushy tail, a scamper up a tree, and there is a squirrel looking down mischievously at you as it clings to a tree branch. Do you know that there were squirrels in our country before Christopher Columbus discovered America? Squirrels are native to every part of the world except Australia and Antarctica.

There are many different kinds of squirrels. Some are red, some are gray, some are black. In tropical countries and in the Orient squirrels are brilliantly colored. There are squirrels with tufted ears, fox squirrels, and flying squirrels, too.

All squirrels are mammals, and they all belong to the rodent family. Rodents are gnawers, and they have extra long sharp teeth in front, two in each jaw. They do not use these to crack nuts as many people think. Squirrels gnaw holes in the hard nut shells to get at the tender nut meat.

Did you ever watch a squirrel hide a nut in the ground and did you wonder if he would ever find it again? Most *naturalists,* as scientists who study animals and plants are called, agree that a squirrel can find a buried nut even when the ground is covered with snow. This does not mean that the squirrel remembers where he has hidden his treasure. It is the squirrel's keen sense of smell that leads him to the buried nut.

21

Flying Squirrel

Red Squirrel

Gray Squirrel

Black Squirrel

Squirrels eat beechnuts, hickory nuts, and almost every other kind of nut. They eat seeds and grain, too. In fine weather, they scurry around, hunting for food that they eat at once or hide for a time when they are again hungry.

Sometimes a red-headed woodpecker will chase a squirrel away

Tufted-ear Squirrel

Summer Home

Winter Home

from its find by pecking at it. The goshawk and the red-tailed hawk also attack squirrels. A squirrel will dodge around the trunk of a tree to escape the claws of a hawk. The gray squirrel flattens out on the side of a tree branch when a hawk appears. Its gray body blends with the bark and is hard to see.

Do you know that some squirrels have summer and winter homes? The summer home is a nest in a tree crotch. The winter home is a hole in a tree and is lined with grass to make it warm and snug. Squirrels often use their winter homes in summer when there is a storm.

Fox Squirrel

23

The gray squirrel builds its nest high in a tree and makes it of twigs and leaves. It likes to live in forests and orchards, but sometimes it may make its home in the trees of a backyard or a city park and it can be fun to watch it eat and play.

The early American pioneers did not like the gray squirrel. Before forests were chopped down to clear land for farms, there were many, many more gray squirrels. As cold wintertime came near, thousands of them gathered together and marched southward. They swam across lakes and rivers and trampled over corn and wheat fields, destroying the crops. Today gray squirrels rarely go south for winter. They usually curl up in a snug tree hole and sleep away much of the cold season.

The noisy, quarrelsome red squirrel lives in the northern part of the United States and in Canada. It nests in a hollow tree and likes to live in pine forests. All through the winter, except in the very coldest weather, you can hear the red squirrel chattering away in the treetops.

Another gray squirrel is called the abert, or tufted-ear, squirrel. If you look at a tufted-ear squirrel quickly from far away, its ears look like a rabbit's. This squirrel makes its home mainly in the mountain forests of Arizona, New Mexico, and Colorado.

The fox squirrel is large and has beautiful fur that varies in color from reddish gray to deep black. Its tail is not as bushy as that of a gray squirrel but it is longer. Most fox squirrels live in the forests of the south but some may be found as far north as Minnesota.

Did you ever see a squirrel fly? If you watch a flying squirrel glide from tree to tree, you may think it is flying but it is not. This squirrel has a thin skin, or *membrane,* on each side of its body. The membrane extends from the front leg to the hind leg and enables the squirrel to glide through the treetops. The flying squirrel lives mostly in trees and comes out only at night.

Did you know that the chipmunk belongs to the squirrel family, too? Scientists call it a ground squirrel. Other ground squirrel cousins of the tree squirrels are the gopher, the marmot, and the prairie dog.

The Busy Beaver

WHEN people are working hard, we sometimes say they are as busy as beavers. Did you ever watch beavers cutting down a sturdy tree or building a dam across a woodland stream or pond? If you have, you know how hard these furry animals can work.

A full-grown beaver measures about three feet from the tip of his nose to the end of his tail. He may weigh as much as sixty pounds but most weigh less. How can a small animal cut down a tall tree?

As the sun rises—for beavers like to work in the cool of early morning or at night when they are safer from their enemies—the beaver leaves his home, or *lodge,* in the water or on the bank of a stream or pond. He selects a tree and begins gnawing busily at the trunk, close to the bottom. His two sharp upper teeth bite into the wood, then his two sharp lower teeth cut away. Chip by chip, the wood is taken out until there is a deep groove all around the tree trunk. When enough cuts have been made, the tree begins to creak and groan. It is about to fall and the beaver rushes out of the way.

Sometimes when a tree is ready to fall, the beaver slaps the ground with his broad, flat tail. This makes a loud spanking sound and warns other beavers of the danger. It is the beaver's way of saying, "Get out of the way!"

After the tree is down, the beaver gnaws off the branches. Then he cuts the tree into lengths which he can drag into the water. Some pieces may be two feet long; others ten or twelve feet.

The branches and logs are very important to the beaver. He uses them in building or repairing his lodge. He uses them also for building and repairing a dam. He also uses them for food, for beavers like to eat the tender, juicy bark of poplar, willow, birch, and other trees.

Did you ever see a beaver lodge? It looks like a huge heap of branches and mud, but it is carefully built. Each branch and stick is put in exactly the right place to help support the dome-shaped roof and the walls that may be three feet thick. Then the beaver carries mud to the lodge by holding it against his body with his front feet. He plasters mud over the branches and sticks to hold them firmly so that the water cannot wash them away.

Inside the lodge is a room about seven feet across and eighteen inches high. It is above the water level and has an air hole in its roof. This is where the beaver family lives and where beaver babies, called *kittens,* are born. The thick walls make the room warm and snug in winter. They help make the lodge safe, too. The only entrance to the room is a tunnel that opens under water. This also helps protect the beavers from animal enemies.

Do you see the beaver swimming toward the underwater pile of branches?

Suppose a beaver sees a wolverine coming. A wolverine is an enemy of the beaver. Quickly the beaver slaps the water with his broad, flat tail. Splash! Splash! The noisy sound warns other beavers in the pond and they swim under water to the tunnel and up into the room. The wolverine cannot follow for he cannot swim under water. If the pond were frozen over, he could walk out on the ice and sniff at the lodge, but the thick walls would keep him out. The beavers still would be safe.

Some beavers dig a second room under the top room and use it for a storehouse for branches and twigs. Other beavers store a pile of branches under water near the tunnel entrance. They stick these firmly in the bottom of the water and sometimes anchor them with stones so they cannot float away. All through the autumn the beavers gather branches and twigs for their storehouse so that when winter comes they will have plenty to eat.

Sometimes a male beaver or a pair of beavers build a lodge and live in it alone, but most beavers live together in a group or *colony*. If there are several families in a pond, they all work together to fill the storehouses and then they all share the food.

Beavers work together to build and repair their dams, too. When the water in a stream or pond is too shallow for a beaver lodge, the beavers build a strong wall of logs and sticks and weight it down with stones and mud. This is a beaver dam. It holds back the water and makes it rise behind the dam. The beavers build the dam higher and higher until the water is just deep enough for their lodges.

All the beavers in a colony help to keep the dam strong. When it is broken, they quickly repair it. At times quite large logs are needed. If there are not enough trees at the edge of a pond, the beavers may dig a canal about a yard wide back into the woods. Then they can float logs out to the pond and the dam.

Beavers are mammals, and beaver babies drink their mother's milk until they are about six weeks old. Then they begin to find their own food. They have watched their mother strip bark from a tree and eat it. Now they try it, too.

There can be from two to six babies in a beaver family each year. A beaver kitten does not have to learn to swim. The webs of skin between the toes of its back feet make swimming easy. Its broad, flat tail acts as a rudder and helps, too. Beavers are more at home in the water than on the land where they have a funny, clumsy walk.

Young beavers like to play, but soon they learn to help with the colony work, too. They live with their parents until they are two years old. Then they find mates and build lodges of their own.

The busy beaver is nature's builder and engineer!

Meet Kitty's Cousins

IT IS hard to believe that a playful kitten has such ferocious cousins as lions, tigers, leopards, jaguars, and lynxes, yet all of these animals are members of the cat family.

Probably Kitty's best-known cousin is the lion of Africa and Asia. A lion sometimes grows to be nearly four feet tall and as long as nine feet from the tip of its nose to the end of its tail. Its loud roar makes most other mammals in the jungle tremble with fear because a lion will attack any but the largest of them. This huge fearless cousin of Kitty's is often called the king of beasts.

All of the cousins in the cat family, from the playful kitten to the king of beasts, are alike in many ways. They all walk, run, crouch, and spring upon their prey in exactly the same way. All of them have five toes on each of their front feet and four on their back feet. These toes have very sharp claws which when they are needed, can be pushed out and used as weapons. Back of the toes and under the balls of the feet are soft cushions which make it easy for them to steal up quietly on their prey.

All members of the cat family use their paws as wash cloths. Like a kitten, a lion licks its paw with its tongue, then wipes it over its face. It laps up water with its tongue, too.

While a kitten's teeth are as sharp as thumbtacks, a lion's teeth are as sharp as daggers. The members of the cat family, like other animals that live on meat, are called

San Diego Zoo

Mother Lion with Cub

carnivores, which means "flesh-eating." All carnivores have sharp teeth and claws.

Only a few animals—a full-grown elephant, a rhinoceros, a hippopotamus, or perhaps a bull buffalo—do not fear the lion. These are the only animals a lion hesitates to attack. These are perhaps the only animals that could escape if a lion did attack them.

A lion rarely climbs trees. It hunts from the ground and pounces upon its prey with enormous strength. Then, holding the animal with its feet, it tears off the flesh with its powerful teeth. If there is more food than the lion can eat at one time, it leaves what it cannot eat. Usually a lion kills only when it is hungry or annoyed. A lion will rarely attack a man if the man makes no move to attack it.

It is hard to see a lion even in the daytime for its brownish-yellow body blends into the color of the tall dry grass around it. However, like other members of the cat family, the lion does most of its hunting at night. All members of the cat family have long thin hairs on the sides of their mouths. These are helpful as feelers in the dark. All of the cat family also have eyes that help them see well in the dark.

A full-grown lion has either a black or yellow mane hanging around his head and shoulders. On the end of his tail is a tuft of black hair, which looks like a brush.

A female lion is smaller than a male lion, and she does not have a mane.

Lions usually live to be about fifteen years old, although some lions

Philip Gendreau

This lion lives in the tall, coarse grass of a prairie, or *savanna*, in Africa.

have been known to live nearly thirty years. Lions normally live in a group called a *pride*. As many as 30 lions live together, including a number of lion babies. The babies, called *cubs*, look and act more like puppies than kittens because they are so chubby. Like other mammal babies, at first they depend upon their mother's milk for food.

Both the father and the mother lion protect the cubs from harm. The mother is even fiercer than the father if any strange animals go near the cubs. If there are many prowlers around, the mother may hide the babies. When the mother lion wants to move one of her cubs, she carries it as any other mother cat would carry her kittens—by taking the skin on the back of the baby's neck in her mouth. In this way she carries her cubs without hurting them.

When they are about a year old, the cubs get their first lessons in hunting. They go stalking through the grass and bushes at night with their mother. They watch as mother sneaks up and attacks some animal that will furnish them with fresh meat. The cubs are not ready to hunt food for themselves until they are at least two years old.

Have you ever watched lions in a circus? The cubs become tame and are easily taught tricks. But lion tamers know that as cubs grow up, they may suddenly become as fierce as wild lions. A trainer knows that he must always be careful when he goes into a lion's cage, for it is difficult to tame the lion, king of the beasts.

Horses, Then and Now

MILLIONS of years ago a strange little four-footed animal no larger than a fox lived on the American continent. It had three toes on each of its hind feet and four toes on its front feet. When it walked, it put its feet flat on the ground with every step. It roamed in herds and lived upon juicy plants.

This odd little creature was only twelve inches high, and it was much smaller and weaker than many of the huge prehistoric beasts that roamed the land at that time. But it was a very important mammal. It was *Eophippus*, the Dawn Horse, the ancestor of our modern horse.

The horse went through many changes and stages of development before it became the horse of today. In the picture above you can see how the horse gradually changed. As scientists have studied the fossil remains in different layers of rock, they have discovered much of the story of the horse from then to now.

How and why did the little Dawn Horse change? We do not know all of the reasons, but we do know many. These little horses did not have claws or sharp teeth to defend themselves. When they were attacked by the huge, meat-eating animals around them, they had to run for their lives.

They could not run very fast on their flat feet so one day the Dawn Horses began running on their toes instead. Then they could

33

run much faster. At any rate, the little horses slowly began to change their ways.

Among living things those that are best fitted to live survive and the weaker ones die. The kinds that are strong or swift or that develop the best ways of protecting themselves from their enemies often become more plentiful, while those that are weak or slow or less well protected are likely to become fewer and finally disappear. In that way living things change.

Of course it takes many hundreds of years for great changes in a species to take place. But the records of the rocks show that the horse began to get larger about the time it started to use its toes. Its jaws and teeth grew stronger, its legs grew longer. As these changes took place all of the horse's toes except one on each foot gradually disappeared. This toe is big and strong, and is surrounded by a horny hoof which is really a very large thick toenail.

As the horse developed, it spread to almost every part of the world, for horses can live in almost every climate. No one knows when man first saw the horse, but on the walls of ancient caves in Europe we can still see pictures of horses that cavemen drew.

The cavemen hunted horses for meat. Later men tamed horses to ride as they hunted other animals. Later still men began to ride horses into battle. In the Middle Ages, knights in heavy armor rode huge, powerful horses. Descendants of those large, sturdy animals are used to pull plows and heavy machinery on farms. They are called draft horses, and some of the best-known kinds are the Belgian, Percheron, Shire, and Clydesdale.

Although the little Dawn Horse lived on the continent of America, horses disappeared from this country before the American Indians came. The first horses the Indians saw were those brought over by the Spanish explorers in the early 1500's.

Some of these horses ran away from their owners. They found grassy plains and clear streams that gave them food and water. As young horses were born and grew up, they formed bands of wild horses. The descendants of these Spanish horses are called mustangs.

At first the Indians of those western plains were afraid of these horses. But soon they learned to capture and tame them. They rode bareback as they shot their bows and arrows and hunted the buffalo or fought other Indian tribes.

The pioneers rode horseback, too, as they settled the country. Horses pulled plows and carriages and stagecoaches. When the settlers moved westward, horses pulled the covered wagons.

Horses even pulled trains until the steam locomotive came into use in the 1830's.

Today cars and trains and planes carry us swiftly from place to place. But we still use horses for work and for pleasure.

Cowboys ride horses as they herd cattle. Usually they ride Quarter Horses, horses that can run swiftly for about a quarter of a mile. The horses are sturdy and sure-footed and can start, turn, and stop at the rider's slightest signal.

At western horse shows, called rodeos, cowboys and horses show their skill in working together.

People still go hunting on horseback. They like to watch horse races and horse shows and polo games. Most of all, people like to ride for pleasure. It is fun to gallop across a field and jump a fence. It is fun to canter along a city bridle path.

That is why we have many kinds of horses today.

Race horses are always Thoroughbreds. All Thoroughbreds are descendants of three famous Arabian stallions that were brought to Europe in the 1700's. They were the Darley Arabian, the Godolphin Barb, and the Byerly Turk. Many hunting and polo horses also have Arabian blood.

Two popular horses for pleasure riding are the American Saddle Horse and the Tennessee Walking Horse. Both are friendly and gentle. They were developed by southern plantation owners who wanted horses that would be fast and yet comfortable to ride. The Morgan is another popular horse for pleasure riding. It is a small horse, but bold and strong and is especially good for riding on rough trails. All Morgan horses are descended from a horse called Justin Morgan, owned by an American schoolteacher in the early 1800's.

Children usually ride ponies. A pony is a small horse that is less than 58 inches or 14.2 hands high. A horse's height is measured in hands from the ground to his withers, the ridge between his shoulder bones. A "hand" is four inches.

A favorite pony for children is the Shetland pony, brought to America from the Shetland Islands, north of Scotland. It is gentle and friendly and not much bigger than a Newfoundland dog.

A stallion is a male horse, and a young male horse is a colt. A mare is a female horse, and a young female horse is a filly. A baby horse is a foal.

Some horses have coats of solid colors such as black, chestnut, bay, white, gray, or golden palomino. Others have coats of mixed colors. Indian ponies often had brown or white spots. These are called "paint ponies" or pintos.

Two very different members of the horse family are the donkey and the zebra. These first came from Asia or Africa.

There are many famous horses in history like *Nelson,* George Washington's horse, and *Traveller,* the horse Robert E. Lee rode.

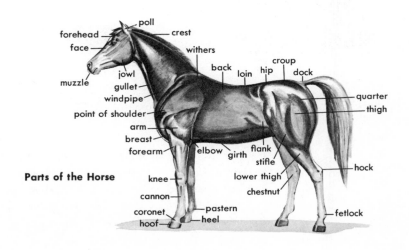

Parts of the Horse

The Mighty Elephant

THE elephant really is an amazing animal. Although it is the largest of all land animals, sometimes weighing more than six tons, it never eats any meat. Its feet are immense, but it can walk so quietly that a person only a short distance away cannot hear the steps. It has a thick skin, but such a poor heating system that it shakes and shivers when the weather is a little chilly. It has two enormous tusks which are really very long upper teeth, although they are of no use in biting.

Probably the strangest thing about an elephant is its trunk. The trunk is both the nose and upper lip stretched to a great length, sometimes as much as seven or eight feet.

It is surprising what an elephant can do with that trunk! He uses it to gather food, sometimes from the ground, sometimes from trees, and often from places several feet to the right or left of where he is standing. He uses it to tear off a huge limb of a tree, or to pick up an object as small as a peanut. He uses it to spurt dust or water over his back. He uses it to test the ground over which he is about to walk, if it might be a dangerous place to step. He uses it to sniff the air and catch the scent of an approaching animal. When he goes swimming or wading, he often uses his trunk as a diver's air tube, by pushing the end of it above the surface for air.

Although the elephant uses his trunk to do many things, he is very careful with it. He rarely fights with it. He uses his tusks and hoofs instead. When he works, he may use his trunk to help steady a load, but usually he does the lifting and carrying with his tusks. Do you see how this Indian elephant is using his trunk and tusks as he carries a log?

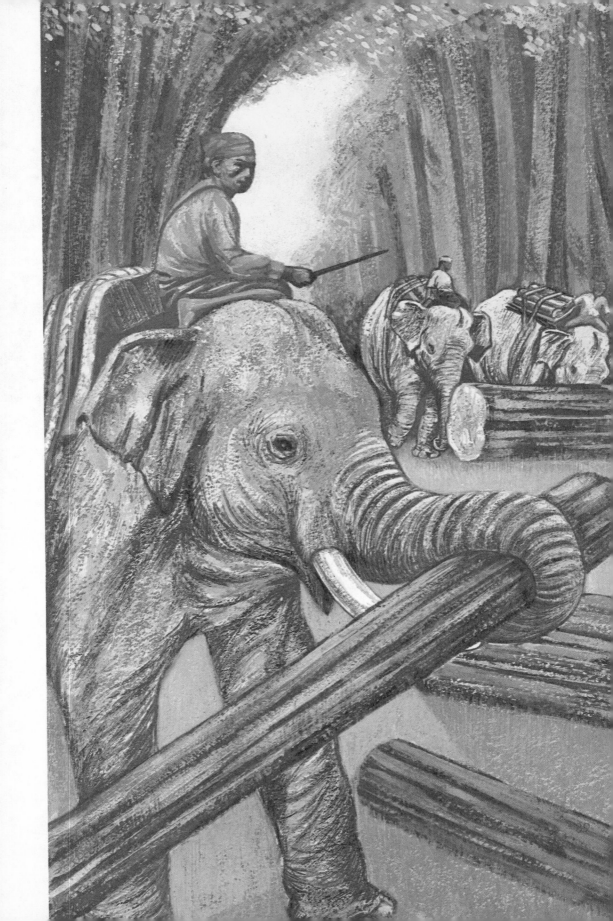

These elephants live on Ceylon, an island in the Indian Ocean. Do you see how placidly they take being bathed? Do you think they like it?

Without a trunk, the elephant would be quite helpless. Probably he would starve, for his neck is so short and thick that he could not bend his head down to eat grass or to get a drink.

The elephant's trunk got its name from the French word, "trompe," which means trumpet. Elephants do make a trumpeting sound through their trunks. The name was changed from trompe to trunk probably through a mistake in spelling. The scientific name is "proboscis."

There are two kinds of elephants, the African and the Indian. The African elephant is found in the warmest parts of Africa, while the Indian elephant is found in southern Asia, and on some islands off the coast of Asia.

The African elephant is the larger of the two kinds. Its large ivory tusks are so valuable that in the past these animals were hunted especially for their tusks.

An African elephant's trunk is wrinkled. Its immense ears hang over its shoulders and almost meet at the back of its head. The ears of the Indian elephant are smaller and its trunk is smoother.

Both elephants have skins that hang in wrinkles and folds down their huge bodies and legs. Even when they are young their skins are wrinkled.

Elephants eat only plants and so they are called *herbivorous* animals. Their main foods are grass and tree branches, but they are fond of such vegetables as beans and carrots. They drink several gallons of water at a time, storing it in their stomachs until it is needed. Their teeth are very good grinders. As the teeth are worn down, they move forward in the jaw and fall out. New teeth then grow in to take the place of the old ones. Elephants sometimes live to be fifty years old, and during that time they may have as many as six new sets of teeth.

This elephant lives in the African jungle. Do you see what big ears he has? They are much bigger than the ears of an Indian elephant.

Philip Gendreau

Although elephants are not meat eaters, they are so huge and powerful that other animals are careful not to make them angry. Even the fiercest wild animal rarely attacks an elephant.

A male elephant is called a *bull.* A female elephant is a *cow,* and a baby elephant is a *calf.* Scientists believe that elephants mate for life.

When a baby elephant is born, it is about two and one-half feet tall and weighs as much as a full-grown man. Its skin is soft, wrinkled, and covered with down. A baby elephant is quite helpless at first. It feeds on milk from its mother's body, although sometimes it is nursed by another mother elephant. Its trunk, which hangs down like a rope, is short and small and of little use. After several months, however, the baby learns to use its trunk as we do our arms. The young elephant grows very slowly. Its mother takes care of it and protects it until it is at least four or five years old. An elephant is about twelve to fourteen years old before it is really grown up.

Elephants live and travel in herds, staying in the same group year after year. There are usually from twenty to forty elephants in a herd, although there may be more. Each herd has a leader, and usually the elephants live peacefully together. Sometimes, however, a bull elephant may go mad. Then he will trample everything in his path. When this happens, the herd forces him to leave and roam by himself. Such an elephant is called a *rogue.*

A herd of elephants usually travels slowly for they are careful to make sure that even the oldest and youngest elephants can keep up.

If a baby elephant is born while a herd is on the march to new grounds, the mother and her baby set the pace for the rest of the trip. When the little fellow gets tired, the entire herd stops and waits for him to rest. When a river must be crossed by swimming, the mother holds him in her trunk. At the same time, an older baby may be climbing on her back, rolling off, then crawling on again. No land mammal is a more expert swimmer than an elephant. A herd may spend an hour at a time in the water splashing and swimming.

Elephants move about mostly at night and sleep standing up during the day. They have such big feet and pillar-like legs that they can keep their balance and get a good rest while standing.

Philip Gendreau

Here is part of a herd of wild African elephants. Do you see how they follow their leader as they travel along?

In captivity, elephants learn to work or perform during the day and to rest lying down at night. A well-trained elephant does not need to be kept in a cage, because it can be trusted to behave well. If an elephant suddenly becomes hard to handle there is usually a good reason. Perhaps its toenails are too long, or the soles of its feet have become too thick and need trimming, or it may be sick. Whatever the trouble may be, the keeper tries to find the cause and give the animal the proper treatment.

Since earliest times elephants have been trained to serve people. Long ago they were used in armies to carry people and supplies, and to frighten the enemy. In India they still are used to do heavy work. They often help with such tasks as loading ships with big timbers and they even swim across rivers with huge loads. No matter what work they are called upon to do, trained elephants usually do it well and obediently.

43

The chimpanzee, the orangutan, the gorilla, the gibbon, and the baboon are all cousins of the monkey.

Monkey Manners

THERE is never a dull moment in the monkey house at the zoo. Monkeys are teasing and chasing one another, making absurd faces at visitors, swinging like trapeze performers, tumbling about in all sorts of ridiculous capers just to attract your attention.

No matter what they may be doing, chattering, scolding, biting, or scratching, monkeys pucker up their faces in the most amusing ways. Sometimes they are like good children, minding their manners in the best style. At other times they seem not to have any manners at all, especially when they rudely pick at one another's fur. But this is not rudeness to them. They are removing little salty pieces of dried skin, and after all they are not given much privacy.

The monkey house is always in such an uproar and topsy-turvy condition that no visitor ever would say monkeys are good house-keepers. However, if you were to see them in their native jungles, you would say at least that they have attractive homes. But there they need to do little about their homes. They only select the site, which always is among branches of trees and hanging vines where flowers and fruits add beautiful bright colors.

Many monkeys live in a camp, either in families or in groups of

45

families. They spend most of their mornings and evenings frolicking. *Swish, swish,* they go through the air, chasing each other, turning somersaults, or swinging their way down from the tall treetops. A mother monkey may have a young one, or sometimes two young ones, hanging on her as she swings from branch to branch.

During the heat of the day, most kinds of monkeys cease much of their chattering and playing and use this quieter time to hunt nuts and fruits for food. Most monkeys rest during the night curled up between branches or in hollow trees.

Monkeys have two hands and two feet. On each hand of most monkeys is a thumb. The feet are almost like hands and are useful in grasping things and in swinging from branch to branch. But while all kinds of monkeys have similar hands and feet, they are different in other ways.

Some monkeys are smaller than squirrels, others are larger than dogs. Some have much hair on their faces, others little or none. Some seem to be wearing bonnets, others fancy collars, while still others have a mane like a lion, or they have a goatee. As for color, almost any color—green, purple, orange, tan, or brown—may be found in monkey land, but some shade of brown is the most common.

American Museum of Natural History

A Howler Monkey in a howling mood.

Monkeys are very skillful in making their way through treetops, especially the American monkeys. It is not unusual for a monkey to leap several feet from tree to tree. When in danger, some of them have been known to leap twenty-five feet through the air. They often perform the most amazing acrobatics with ease at heights of a hundred feet or more.

Spider

Howler

Marmoset

Rhesus

Guereza

Moustache

Diana

Monkeys that live in Central and South America are called New World monkeys.
Those that live in Africa and southwestern Asia are called Old World monkeys.
The three monkeys at the top of this page belong to the New World. Do you see
how they swing by their very long tails? Old World monkeys have shorter tails.

Scientists believe the chimpanzee is the most intelligent of all animals except man. This "chimp," called Enos, was five years old when the picture was taken. He was a test pilot, used in the early days of the space program to test how man would be able to perform certain tasks in space.

U.S. Air Force Photo

Even the young monkeys follow their parents in all these antics as soon as they can. The parents do not seem in the least concerned about the reckless stunts their young perform high up in the treetops.

Some people keep monkeys for pets. The woolly monkey makes the best pet, because it is usually better natured than the others. The capuchin is one of the monkeys which often helps the organ grinder entertain boys and girls, by dancing around, making funny faces and bowing handsomely when a coin is dropped in the basket. It gets its name from a band of fur under its chin which makes it appear to be wearing a capuchin monk's hood.

The gentle and friendly marmoset is only about eight inches tall. It has soft fluffy fur and a long bushy tail. A marmoset seems to enjoy eating cockroaches and spiders.

The owl monkey is sometimes kept as a pet in Brazil. Its face looks much like that of an owl. It is the only monkey that rests in the daytime and hunts food at night.

The squirrel monkey has a pleasant disposition and cries to be held and petted. The spider monkey is the most intelligent of all the monkeys. But the rhesus monkey is the one most often seen at the circus, and as a pet. This is because the rhesus is more easily raised and can stand cold weather better than other kinds of monkeys. Like other monkeys, it eats fruits, vegetables, insects, and spiders.

The howling monkey is the largest as well as the noisiest of all American monkeys. There is a brown howler and a yellow one and a red one. They all have surly manners, and all make harsh noises.

Like the other apes—the gibbon, the orangutan, the chimpanzee— the gorilla is a close relative of the monkey. A full-grown gorilla may be six feet tall and weigh more than 400 pounds. In its native home in Central Africa, it will usually get out of the way of man. But in captivity or when pursued, a gorilla can be very dangerous. This gorilla is beating his chest in anger!

The baboon is another kind of monkey. It lives on the ground among the rocks and hills and runs swiftly on all fours. It has large cheek pouches which it fills with food before it swallows. Baboons feed in herds and eat fruits, roots, birds' eggs, and insects. The face and buttocks of some baboons may be bright blue, pink, or scarlet.

Moles, the Master Diggers

LOOKING at the picture on this page, you may wonder what caused the zigzag ridges on the lawn. If you were to dig down below one of the ridges, you would find that a small tunnel has been burrowed through the ground. The animal that makes this tunnel is a mole.

Most people have never seen moles, for the little animals spend most of their time underground, just digging. If they did not do that, they would be very hungry because they need so much food. If we could weigh all of the insects and worms that a mole eats in one day and night we would find that their weight amounts to more than one fourth of its own weight. Moles belong to a group of animals called *insectivores*, which means "insect eating."

When the ground is dry, the mole works several feet underground because then earthworms and many of the insects go down where there is moisture. If the ground is wet so that the animals it eats are near the top, it burrows just below the surface and then it leaves the ridges on lawns, gardens, or fields. But moles are helpful to us, too, because they eat so many harmful insects.

Moles are only about six inches long, or about the size of little kittens that have just opened their eyes. They have such a good method of digging that they may go across a small yard in a single night. Near the surface where the earth is loose, the mole pushes the dirt up with one of its strong paws, using the other paw to push its body forward. Deeper down where the ground is packed, one paw at a time is used in digging and pushing the dirt back.

Moles do not have good eyes and ears. In fact, you would not be able to find a mole's ears at all, although the animals are able to hear sounds. Their eyes are about as small as a pinhead, and are well protected by fur. Scientists believe that moles only are able to tell light from dark. But moles have a good sense of smell by which they know where the insects and earthworms are.

Mole fur is very soft and thick and, even though the mole spends most of its life underground, the fur is very clean. Dirt does not get into it because the tiny hairs are placed so closely together. Because the fur is so fine, soft, and beautiful in color, it is often used for trimmings on dresses and coats. Some moles are black, some are yellowish-gray, some are brown, and sometimes even a white one is found.

Even if a mole is small, it is very ferocious. Living underground it is well protected, but it can, when necessary, fight a furious and stubborn battle using its sharp teeth and claws as weapons to overcome an enemy. The weasel is one of its enemies. A mole may fight other moles, too, sometimes. A mole may attack a person if its home is disturbed.

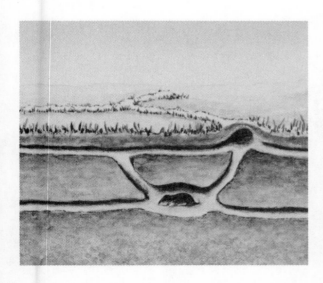

In this picture you can see the underground tunnels a mole makes. A nest, or *burrow*, is in the bottom tunnel. A mother mole builds her nest of roots and grasses in one of the deeper tunnels. There, three or four hairless babies are born early in the spring. Like other mammal babies, they are helpless at first and need much care. When they are about five weeks old, young moles begin to dig their own food. The father mole does not live with the family.

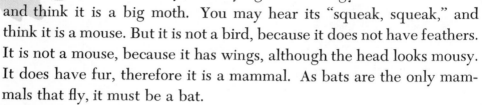

A Bat, Not a Bird

YOU may see it flying through the air and think it is a bird. You may see it flying around a light and think it is a big moth. You may hear its "squeak, squeak," and think it is a mouse. But it is not a bird, because it does not have feathers. It is not a mouse, because it has wings, although the head looks mousy. It does have fur, therefore it is a mammal. As bats are the only mammals that fly, it must be a bat.

In the evening bats fly around lights to catch insects. All our American bats are insectivores. Since there are usually so many insects flying around lights, we know that those are good places for bats to find their food. A bat darts this way and that way catching gnats, flies, and mosquitoes. In the mouselike mouth they are cut and ground by the many sharp teeth before being swallowed. Bats remove the hard shell-like wings of June bugs and other beetles and eat only the soft parts of them. You would have a hard time catching enough insects to feed a bat. If you could weigh all the insects a bat catches in one night, you would be surprised to find they weigh half as much as the bat itself.

A baby bat goes on insect hunting trips, too, although it does not eat any insects. You would not expect it to eat insects, because bats are mammals and all mammal babies are fed milk from their mothers' bodies. Mother bats

Common Brown Bat.

usually have only one or two baby bats at one time, although some-times there are as many as four. They all cling to her fur and body and go sailing through the air everywhere she goes. They are really very big babies and four of them weigh as much as their mother. How she can carry such a heavy load is hard to understand.

When they are big enough, the mother hangs the babies upside down in a safe place and leaves them to go out and hunt for food. A baby bat does not mind hanging upside down when it sleeps. The father and mother bat also sleep that way. Each hind foot has five toes with sharp, curved claws which hook over branches like clothes hangers over a rod. One of the claws is very much like a thumb. When the weather is warm, you may find a bat hanging up-side down, taking a daytime snooze in a dark corner of some deserted building, in the hay loft of a barn, or in almost any out-of-the-way place. Not all bats stay close to peoples' homes. Many of them live in woods or in caves with other bats.

Bats have fingers as long as their bodies and when flying, are able to use them very well. Their wings are made of a thin fold of skin stretched from finger to finger; from finger to the arm and body; from the

Century

finger, arm and body to the hind leg, and on to the tail. In this way the fingers, arms, legs, and tail help to make good wings. The wings fold up against the body when the animal rests just as an umbrella is folded when it is put down. In flight, the wings enable the bat to dart and glide with the swiftness of a swallow. The fold of skin has many little nerves in it and is very sensitive to touch and vibration.

We do not like to have untrue stories told about our friends. Bats have untrue stories told about them, and they are our friends because they eat harmful insects. Perhaps you have heard someone say "blind as a bat." Bats are not blind, although their eyes are small. A bat is sometimes accused of carrying unpopular insects, such as bedbugs, into peoples' homes but that is not so. You may have heard, too, about bats flying in women's hair, but that also is untrue. Bats have such a

53

perfect sense of control in flying that they do not run into people, and there is nothing about a bat of which anyone needs to be afraid.

Bats make excellent use of a kind of radar that is all their own. They are able to fly in the darkest night—when their eyes cannot be of much help to them—among buildings, trees, and even wires, without hitting any of these things. They have a very good way of doing this. As they fly, they cry out in a high pitch. Although people cannot hear these sounds, bats' ears detect them very well. If anything is in the way, their cries echo back to them. In this way they can tell where the object is and avoid bumping into it.

During the winter bats find a warm place, crawl into it and hibernate, coming out only when it is warm enough to find insects. They do not always hibernate near their summer home but may travel a long way before finding a suitable place. A bat may choose a hollow log or a tree trunk, or it may go into a cave and spend the winter there with hundreds of other bats. The Carlsbad Caverns in New Mexico are famous as a home for bats.

There are several kinds of bats in North America. The kinds you may see are the big and little brown bats, red bats, large-eared bats, hoary bats, and the little, free-tailed ones. Some of them are easily known by their color. Hoary bats are brown with a frosty tip on their fur. Red bats are bright reddish brown. Large-eared bats are grayish brown. The little free-tailed ones are like their name. The common brown bat is about four inches long and its wings measure about twelve inches from tip to tip. That is the bat you are most likely to see flying about in the evening.

These hibernating bats were taken from deep in an unused limestone mine in Illinois. They sleep soundly as they are poured into a box for shipment to hospitals, medical schools, and laboratories where they will be used for research.

A Sea Going Mammal

MOST PEOPLE when asked to name the largest mammal, say it is the elephant. But many whales are ten times as large as any elephant. Even baby whales may weigh more than full-grown elephants. Some whales' heads are as big as an elephant's whole body.

Although they live in oceans, whales are mammals, just as many land animals are. Their bodies are in many ways like fishes' bodies. They are streamlined like fish. They swim with their tails as fishes do and their front legs, or flippers, look like the fins of a fish. Whales have no back legs or flippers, but some of them have fins on their backs just as fishes have. It is not surprising that many people think whales are a kind of fish.

They are mammals because the mother whales feed their babies milk from their bodies, just as land mammals nurse their young. Also, instead of having gills as fish have, they have lungs such as land mammals have. It is true that the bodies of whales are not covered with hair as the bodies of most land mammals are, but while they are very young they do have some hair.

If you look at the picture above, you will see something that looks like a fountain. It is really a whale "spouting" or blowing the air out of his lungs. As the air is pushed out in a big puff, any water above it is pushed up, and also some of the moisture in his breath may condense or turn to water. The spout, caused by the puffing of air out of a whale's lungs, is sometimes fifteen feet high. As soon as the stale air is blown out, the whale breathes in fresh air as we do. He must keep

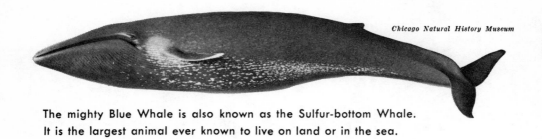

The mighty Blue Whale is also known as the Sulfur-bottom Whale.
It is the largest animal ever known to live on land or in the sea.

his nose above the water until his lungs are filled with air again.

Baby whales can swim when they are born. They follow their mothers through the water, although they are not looking for food as she is. They depend upon their mother's milk for food. Mother whales have large milk glands because their babies are big and need a great deal of milk. A baby whale is called a calf. But it does not look much like a calf you see on a stock farm.

Under the gray or black skin of whales is a layer of fat. The fat protects the animals from the cold. It also protects them from the bite of other animals and from the heavy pressure of the water when they go down deep. Sometimes the layers of fat are almost two feet thick. Whales would not be nearly as large if they did not have so much fat.

Not all whales eat the same things, because not all whales have teeth. Some have plates of whalebone which hang down from the roofs of their mouths. These plates have fringes along their edges. The fringes act as strainers to catch many small animals such as crabs, jellyfish, and mollusks. Often plants are caught. When the mouth is full, the huge tongue, which may weigh as much as half a ton, is raised against all these plants and animals and the water is squeezed out, leaving masses of food. The food is swallowed down a tube, or gullet, which goes to the stomach.

Whales which have teeth, have much bigger throats. The teeth may be a foot long and ten inches around. Some kinds of whales have teeth both on the upper and lower jaws but others have teeth only on the lower jaws. Whales with teeth and big throats eat bigger animals such as giant squids, cuttlefish, and penguins.

The Hump-back Whale is named that because it humps its back when it is about to sound.

The Sperm Whale is a fierce fighter. These whales often have crushed whaling boats and ships.

American Museum of Natural History Photos

The Right Whale was hunted almost to extinction because it was easy to overtake and gave so much oil and whalebone.

The largest whales are the blue whales. They are not only the largest mammals, but they are the largest of all animals known to have lived on land or sea. One of those caught measured 106 feet, that length being about the length of six automobiles, placed bumper to bumper. Blue whales have whalebone plates instead of teeth.

Sperm whales look as though they had had their noses bumped. The heads are very large, blunt, and shaped like a barrel. These whales have a mixture of oil and waxy substance in them which has many uses. As much as 100 barrels of this oil, and twenty-four barrels of the waxy substance, has been taken from one whale about sixty feet long. On the lower side of a sperm whale's head is a long and narrow mouth with many sharp teeth on the lower jaw. Sperm whales, unlike blue whales, do not spout or blow fountains straight upward. They spout the air and water mist forward from their heads.

Right whales got their name because they yielded so much oil and whalebone that they were considered the right whales for the whalers to catch. They have big heads, almost half as long as their whole bodies. Some of their whalebone plates hang down in their mouths as much as six or seven feet.

A hundred years ago, whaling was a much more important industry than it is now. Then the oil was widely used for lighting people's homes. Whales were already becoming scarcer when petroleum products and, later, electric lights took the place of the old whale oil lamps. However, whale oil still has many uses.

In the old whaling days, sailing vessels with small boats and other equipment went on cruises that sometimes lasted two or three years, or until the men had a shipload of whale products. When a whale was seen, boats were lowered and men rowed out toward it. At the right distance, a harpoon, a large spear with barbs on it, was thrown with great force into the whale's body.

Attached to the harpoon was a long rope lying in coils at the bottom of the boat. As the whale tried to escape the rope would be pulled out at great speed. Often the animal would turn back and attack one of the boats and sometimes upset it with his powerful tail. But if the harpoon and rope held and everything went well, the whale would be forced to give up after a long struggle. Then the men would tow it to the ship. There the oil and whalebone would be taken out. After its removal the rest of the whale's body was left to be eaten by the birds and other animals.

Today newer ways of catching whales, such a shooting the harpoon from a cannon on a large ship, make whaling easier and more efficient. Because of these modern whaling methods, whales have become very scarce and more is being done to protect them. Citizens of the United States, for example, are prohibited by law from whaling or importing whale products.

The Finback Whale is about 60 feet long. It is the most common whale.

L. Chace

Whales travel from one ocean to another, sometimes making long journeys. Several may go together, or they may travel alone. Although whales may be found in almost all oceans, they are usually found in cold waters.

Arctic Terns

BIRDS

Champion Travelers

ALL THE birds that travel north for the summer and south for the winter are called migratory birds. The highways which they follow in the sky are called migratory routes. The word *migratory* comes from the word *migrate* which means to travel from one place to another to live.

No one can be sure why birds migrate. Some scientists think that birds have an instinct, or in-born feeling, to migrate, because long ago it became necessary for them to travel in order to get enough food. Some believe that the migration of birds was caused by a great change in the climate. Others believe birds began to migrate because there were too many of them feeding in the same places.

Now, because their ancestors long ago lived in certain places, birds return to those places every year, either to make their nests or to spend the winter. Scientists also say that the change in the length of day is part of the reason why birds migrate. But none of these reasons explains why some birds migrate and others do not. Perhaps sometime you may help to answer the question of why birds migrate.

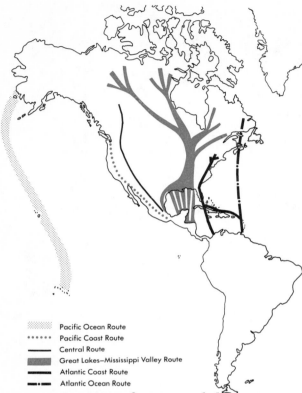

Pacific Ocean Route
Pacific Coast Route
Central Route
Great Lakes—Mississippi Valley Route
Atlantic Coast Route
Atlantic Ocean Route

There are six sky highways which most birds take when they migrate. The arctic tern travels the Atlantic Ocean route, the bobolink, the Atlantic Coast route. More birds take the Mississippi River Valley route than any other, probably because it is safer than the others.

Perhaps you may wonder how birds find their way along these sky highways. It may be that the mountains, rivers, and coastlines serve as sign posts for some of them. It may be that some birds follow the route where food is most easily found.

Some birds, such as the arctic tern, fly long distances over water. Neither the landmark answer nor the food answer solves the mystery or how the terns find their way. Most scientists think that birds have a "sense of direction" which tells them the way to go.

There is another mystery about the migration of birds. It always takes place at about the same time of year. Robins and bluebirds arrive in Chicago early in March. Cedar waxwings arrive in a little town in Iowa on almost the same date in April, year after year, on their way farther north to their summer homes. The birds that arrive in May come from much farther south, and although it takes them longer, they come at about the same time each year.

Scientists believe that birds follow a schedule which makes it easy for them to get food while they travel. They must need much food then because they use up so much energy. If the birds eat seeds or insects from the ground, they are likely to travel by night and spend their days resting and eating. Thrushes, vireos, orioles, and bobolinks are night fliers. Many fliers eat insects that are in the air. They open their mouths and catch the insects that fly in front of them. Swallows, martins, nighthawks, and swifts are day fliers. Some water birds migrate either by day or by night.

For a long time people did not know about migration. They explained the absence of many birds in the fall and winter in queer ways. Some people thought they hibernated in the mud as frogs do, while others thought the birds flew to the moon. The reason people believed that birds flew to the moon was that they saw the night fliers flying in the moonlight.

Bird banding has taught people many things about bird migration. A bird is caught in a bird trap or cage. Then a very light band with a number on it is put around one of the bird's legs. A record is made showing the date, place, kind of bird, and the number on the band. This is reported to an office in Washington, D. C. Then the bird is turned loose again. Perhaps that same bird is caught somewhere another time. The person who catches it sees that it is wearing a band. He makes another record showing the date, place, kind of bird, and the number on the band and again turns the bird loose. This record is also sent to Washington.

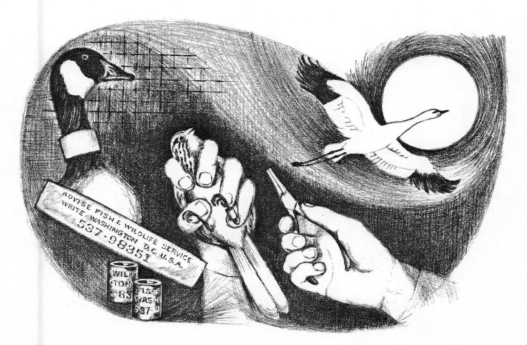

An arctic tern might be banded on May 18 off the coast of Brazil and the same number might be reported June 16 from Greenland. Scientists would then know that between May 18 and June 16 this bird had traveled from Brazil to Greenland. Whenever a banded bird is found, the bird's number should be reported to the office in Washington.

Although scientists agree that birds can get more and better food because they migrate, they also know that migration trips are dangerous for the birds. There always is the danger of storms when birds may become blinded, lose their way, and be blown against tall buildings or other obstacles. There also is the danger that the birds may not be strong enough to make the trip. Although most birds prepare for these long journeys, some may not be able to keep up with the rest.

Another danger for migrating birds, especially ducks and geese, is that they may be shot by hunters who watch for them along the way.

The bobolinks are among the first birds to leave the north for the south. Their flight is not a continuous one. The first stop is in the marshes of Delaware, New Jersey, Maryland, and Virginia. Even the western birds fly east to join the ones in the Atlantic States before going south. In this region they are known as reed birds.

The next stop is in the rice fields of the Carolinas. There they help themselves so freely to the rice that they are called rice birds. Later stops are made in Cuba and Jamaica. By the time they reach the plains and marshes of the Paraguay River, they are so well fed that people call them butter birds.

Canada geese usually fly in a broad V-shaped line, with a leader at the head and guards in the rear.

The Canada Goose nests in northern parts of the United States and as far north as there are trees in Canada. It makes day and night flights. It usually stops in its day flights at sunset. This is done to feed upon the reeds and sedges of some pond or lake, or upon the wheat, corn, or other grains that have fallen in a farm field.

Canadian Geese

Black and White
Warbler

Bobolink

Arctic Tern

Golden Plover

Many states have passed laws which forbid the shooting of these birds at certain seasons. Migrating birds must also watch out for birds and other animals that are their enemies.

Birds are champion travelers, but the arctic tern is the champion of all bird travelers. It spends nearly half of every year traveling. Every spring it flies from its winter home near the South Pole to its summer home near the North Pole. Every fall it flies back to the South Pole again. This makes a distance of about 22,000 miles which the arctic tern travels every year.

About the last of August it leaves the cold country of the north. Flying southward it crosses the hot region near the equator and flies on until it reaches another very cold part of the earth near the South Pole. This is its home during the three months that the sun shines there practically all through the day and night. Then it travels back 11,000 miles to return to its nesting place in the far north. If the tern had a speedometer on its body, it would probably register about 150 miles a day on these long trips.

Arctic terns arrive back at their northern home early in June. During the next three months while they are near the North Pole, they again have almost constant daylight.

This long summer day is a busy one for the birds. They must make their nests and raise their families. It isn't necessary to spend much time building a nest, because the nest is very simple. It is only a hollow place in the sand, lined with dry grass or sea weed. Three greenish-white eggs spotted with brown, black, and lavender are laid in the nest.

Although you might wonder how the baby birds ever live, the terns seem to do very well raising their families in the cold of the far north. Some of the birds have been found in nests with snow banked all around them. However, not all arctic terns make their nests quite so far north.

The terns living in the far north eat mostly fish because any other foods would be difficult to find in that region.

The tern has webbed feet and pointed wings and tail. The bluish gray color of its body makes it hard to be seen in the air, or over sand, snow, or water.

Another bird famous for its travels is the golden plover which makes its nest in the northern part of North America. It migrates 2,000 miles across the ocean to South America, and then 2,000 miles across South America to Argentina. The most surprising thing about the golden plover is that it flies back to its summer home by a different route, going back almost entirely over land.

The bobolink makes its nest in the northern part of the United States, and spends its winters in the central part of South America.

Some birds travel fast, others take their time. The black and white warbler travels very slowly on its migratory trip. It spends about seventy-seven days on the way and averages less than twenty-five miles a day. It spends its winters in Cuba and Central America, and makes its nest in the region south of Hudson Bay.

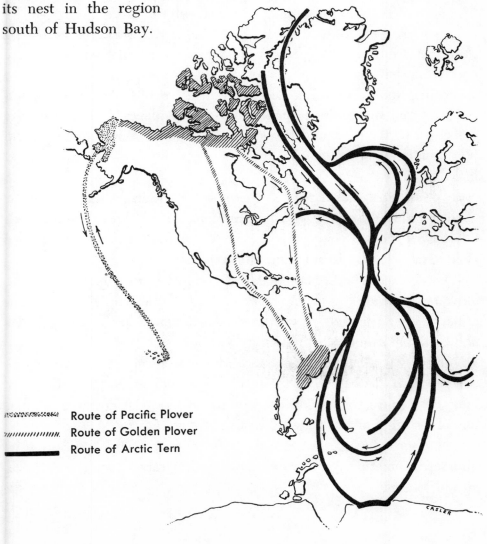

mmmmmmmm **Route of Pacific Plover**
mmmmmmmm **Route of Golden Plover**
━━━━━━ **Route of Arctic Tern**

The Friendly Robin

"CHEER UP! Chee, chee, chee!" sings the friendly robin as he nests close to your home. If you look out of your window, you might see a robin, for these birds nest almost everywhere in the United States. The robin has a reddish breast and is often called Robin Redbreast. His head is dark and his throat is striped black and white. The rest of his body is gray. As a robin flies, you can catch a glimpse of white under his tail feathers. The ends of the outer tail feather are also white.

Like most birds, the father robin has brighter colors than the mother robin. Her duller colors protect her when she sits on her nest to lay and hatch the eggs.

Mother Robin builds her nest firmly. In her bill she carries leaves, twigs, string, and scraps of paper to a chosen place. Then she carries wet mud to the nest and turns and twists until the mud binds the other materials together. When the nest is done, it is firm and shaped like a bowl.

A robin's nest may have four, five, or six greenish-blue eggs in it. Mother Robin sits on the eggs for fourteen days until they are hatched. She leaves the nest only once a day to get food and water. Father Robin stays nearby to sing and entertain her.

When baby robins are hatched, they have almost no feathers. About all you can see are big yellow mouths. Both Father and Mother Robin are kept busy bringing cutworms and earthworms to thrust down the babies' mouths and feed the hungry young birds.

The baby robins grow fast. In about eleven days they are almost covered with feathers. But they still do not look much like robins, for their breasts are spotted. They look much like thrushes at this time, for robins are part of the wood thrush family.

A mother robin raises more than one family of baby robins in a summer. Sometimes she raises as many as three families of birds in one season.

It is interesting to watch young robins leave the nest for the first time. They are ready when their wing feathers are big enough, even though their tails are short. Some of the young robins perch on the sides of the nest for several minutes before they are brave enough to take off. At first they flutter among the low branches or on the ground. Father and Mother Robin chatter excitedly from higher perches as if to say, "Be careful, be very careful. Watch out for a cat." After a few attempts, the young birds use their wings better but have trouble keeping their balance because of their stubby tail feathers. But by fall they have wings and tails as good as their father and mother have. They need strong wings and tails to make their trip south.

Every year robins move south in the fall. If you live in the central part of the United States you may have robins in your yard all winter. But your winter robins probably are not those that were there in the summer. In the fall, soon after the robin family in your yard takes off to go farther south, other robins from the north may choose your yard for their winter home. Every robin has its summer home and its winter home.

Do you know on what date last spring the robins arrived in your yard? If you do, then you will know when to expect them from the south next spring. People wonder how robins keep their calendars

L. Chace

While robin eggs are hatching, the mother bird leaves the nest only once a day to find food and water. As she sits on the eggs and keeps them warm, the baby birds begin to grow inside the shells. When an egg is ready to hatch, the baby bird pecks with its special egg-tooth on the shell wall. As it pecks, the shell begins to crack and a hole appears. When the hole is big enough, the bird sticks its head out. Then it struggles until the shell breaks and the bird is out!

Philip Gendreau

because they always seem to arrive so promptly each year. But a robin's calendar seems to be its own secret. Robins sometimes return to the same homes year after year.

The robins are not very welcome in places where there are cherry orchards. They probably would not take so many cherries from the trees if there were mulberries or other wild fruits nearby for them to eat. For every cherry robins eat, they will eat at least one grasshopper and two beetles. When the cherries are gone, the robins will eat even more grasshoppers and beetles.

Have you ever watched a robin tip its head from one side to another as if to say, "What do I hear?" Then seen it suddenly thrust its bill into the ground and come up with a worm in it? Perhaps it was a cutworm. Thus whenever you hear someone say a robin took his cherries you may be sure that the robin earned some of them because he also had eaten many harmful worms and insects.

Years ago robins were sometimes used to make stews or meat pies. Today most people would not think of killing this friendly bird with the cheerful song of Cheer up! Cheer up! Chee, chee, chee.

Flicker

Hairy

Pileated

Ivory-Billed

Sapsucker

The Woodpecker's Peck

AMONG the best known bird families in the United States is the woodpecker family. In many ways its members are much alike. They all have very sharp, strong bills and short, stubby tails. Their legs are short, and most woodpeckers have four toes on each foot, two of them pointing forward and two of them pointing backward. Most woodpeckers are black and white trimmed with red. The arctic three-toed woodpecker, however, has three toes on each foot and yellow trim instead of red. The flicker, another woodpecker, also has some yellow, and is more brown than black.

Most woodpeckers eat insects, insect eggs, and insect caterpillars. They hold on to the sides of trees or poles with their toes, and brace their bodies with their tails. Then *peck, peck, peck,* they go, as they work away on the wood in front of them. Their bills are like chisels. They take out little chips of wood as they cut their way into the tree or pole.

Soon the woodpecker reaches an insect which it brings out with its long tongue. A woodpecker's tongue is three or four times as long as its beak and is barbed on the end. The insect does not have much of a chance to escape.

It is fun to watch how skillfully a woodpecker goes about its work. Up a tree it goes, tapping here and there as it hitches its way along, stopping now and then to pick up some insect eggs; but all the while, listening, listening, listening, for the sound of a borer within. Woodpeckers always seem to drill the holes in just the right places. They often are called "friends of the forests" by the

NEST

RED-HEADED

people who know them. It is a good name to give to the woodpeckers because they eat so many insects that are very harmful to trees.

However, certain members of the woodpecker family, such as the sapsuckers, sometimes kill trees because they make too many holes in them. They do not search for insects but are after fresh sap to drink. Sapsuckers' tongues are not as long as those of other woodpeckers. Their tongues have a brush on the end with which they gather the sap. Because they harm trees instead of helping them, sapsuckers are sometimes called the "woodpecker bad boys."

Sometimes, after woodpeckers have pecked and chipped their way into the insects' homes, they keep on pecking and chipping, pecking and chipping, until the holes have become big enough for the bird carpenters themselves to go inside. There they may work until the holes are a foot deep and lined with very fine chips at the bottom.

71

This is the way that most woodpeckers make their nests.

Four or five white eggs are laid on the bed of chips at the bottom of a nest. When the babies hatch, they look like many other baby birds with their little pink, naked bodies and big beaks and mouths. The mother and father birds feed them from their sharp chisel-like bills, which look as though they might jab right through the babies. The parents, however, are simply feeding their young ones insects and larvae which form most of their food.

Many woodpeckers stay in the north during the whole year. The hole in which the babies spent the summer makes a nice warm home for the grown birds during the winter.

The ivory billed woodpecker, so-called because its bill looks like ivory, is the largest of the American woodpeckers. It is almost two feet long, and it lives in very dense forests of cypress trees. There are few of these forests left and that is partly the reason that there are almost no ivory billed woodpeckers left. Occasionally, people who live in Florida or Alabama see one in the cypress forests there.

The pileated woodpecker is almost as big, and also is very scarce. It usually lives in dense forests of evergreen trees. There are still more evergreen forests than there are cypress forests and so we have more pileated woodpeckers than ivory billed ones.

The Downy woodpecker, which is only about six inches long, is the smallest of the American woodpeckers. Many Downy woodpeckers may be found because they are not particular about what kinds of trees they live in. Hairy woodpeckers look very much like Downy wood-peckers but they are a little larger. Hairy woodpeckers do not have black spots on their white tail feathers as Downy woodpeckers have. Downy and hairy seem like strange names for these birds because there is nothing downy or hairy about either of them.

The red headed woodpecker and the flicker are two of our best known woodpeckers. They are very friendly. The flicker, especially, makes friends not only with other woodpeckers but also with robins, bluebirds, and sparrows.

There are more than twenty kinds of woodpeckers. All are easily recognized by their *peck, peck, peck,* by their colors, and by their chisel-like beaks.

L. Chace

A Bird that Cannot Fly

THE ostrich is the largest bird in the world, but it cannot fly. Some scientists believe that once, many thousands of years ago, the ostrich could fly like other birds. Then slowly a change began.

The ostrich has a huge body. This made it difficult for the bird to lift off the ground quickly.

The ostrich has long, strong legs. The big bird began to use its legs more and more. As it did so, it found that it could run faster than it could fly.

At any rate, so scientists believe, ostriches began to run more and fly less. Their wings grew less and less able to carry them. Finally, after thousands of years, the ostrich lost the power to fly in the air.

Ostriches still use their wings as a help in getting up speed when they start to run. They also use them in turning and stopping, much like an airplane pilot uses ailerons and flaps. Ostriches have been known to run at the rate of forty-five miles an hour. This is faster than horses can run.

These huge birds stand as tall as a horse and sometimes weigh as much as 300 pounds. In Africa, their native land, they often are seen with some of the larger mammals. The zebra, which is also a fast runner, seems to be one of their favorite companions.

Imagine waiting half an hour for a boiled egg in the morning, and when it is served, having egg enough to serve a dozen people. Each ostrich egg weights about as much as two dozen chicken eggs, or three pounds. Ostrich eggs are delicious and often are used for food by people in Africa.

73

For a nest, ostriches simply scoop out a shallow place in the warm sand. Although about fifteen eggs usually are laid in a nest, there may be as many as fifty. The number depends on how many mates the father bird has. Sometimes as many as five or six mother birds may lay eggs in the same nest.

The sun and the warm sand usually keep the eggs warm enough during the daytime. But one of the mother ostriches may sit on the eggs and watch over them during the day. The feathers on the under part of the mother birds' bodies are white but above, where they show most, they are dull gray— almost the color of the sand around them. This makes it hard for them to be seen and so helps to protect the nest from harm.

At night, the father ostrich sits

on the nest. The feathers on the under part of his body are white like those of the mother, but those on the rest of his body are black. He, too, is not easily seen and because of his color he is better able to protect the nest during the night.

In about six or seven weeks the baby ostriches hatch. At first they are about the size of full-grown chickens. When they are a few hours old they are able to follow their parents as they hunt for food.

L. Chace

Ostriches eat mostly plant parts, such as green leaves, stems, seeds, and fruits.

The babies grow very fast. In six months they are almost as big as their parents, although they really are not grown-up until they are three years old. The feathers of the young birds are a dull yellow, streaked with a darker tinge. They are not nearly as beautiful as those of their parents. The long beautiful plumes do not appear until the young birds are full-grown.

The father ostrich does not sing to his mates as many other birds do, because the only sound he can make is more like a lion's roar than a bird's song. But he struts and shows off before them. Fluffing up his feathers, he holds his wings like an open fan, then struts around as much as to say, "See how beautiful I am!"

The members of an ostrich family seem to get along well together. A father bird can be very fierce if he needs to protect his nest or his mates. A kick from his strong legs is as powerful as a horse's kick.

Some people who have lived in Africa have seen ostriches dance, or "waltz." At the beginning of the dance several birds run for a few steps beside one another, then suddenly stop, raise their wings, and whirl around and around waving their beautiful plumes. Sometimes the dancers get so dizzy that they have to stagger out of the dance.

Nowadays there are not as many ostriches as there were some years ago, because many of the birds have been killed for their beautiful plumes. Some people have made a business of raising ostriches. Their ostrich farms have big pens or fields with high fences around them in which to keep the birds. A father and several mother birds are kept in each pen. They are fed chopped beets, cabbage, oranges, and corn. The baby ostriches are fed wet foods, alfalfa, and other green plants.

Once or twice a year the birds' large plumes are clipped off, but new ones soon grow out. The plumes sell for a good price. They are often used on women's hats and for costumes and other decorations. As some ostriches live to be eighty years old, each bird may furnish many plumes during its lifetime.

Sometimes ostriches are called "camel birds" because they are in many ways like camels. Their long scrawny necks and legs do make one think of a camel. Except for the plumes of the birds, some people think they are almost as homely as camels. They, too, can go a long time without water. Ostriches, also, are somewhat stupid, often eating such harmful things as nails, buttons, and pieces of wire. Even when tame, they never become very friendly with people.

American Museum of Natural History

Kiwi

The ostrich has many relatives, the rhea of South America, often called the American ostrich, the emu and cassowary of Australia, and the kiwi of New Zealand. All are smaller than the ostrich, especially the kiwi, which is no larger than a good-sized hen. The kiwi is an odd bird, having no tail at all, and very tiny wings. And, like the ostrich, these birds, too, have forgotten how to fly.

A Fancy Flier

THE tiny, fleet hummingbird is the smallest of all North American birds and certainly one of the strangest. It can fly, like a helicopter, straight up in the air, backwards as though in reverse, and it can stop any place in midair and stay suspended. When it flies straight ahead it can go

Paul Guillimette, Inc.

a mile a minute. It cannot walk or run. Its tiny feet are suitable only for perching on fine twigs.

This little fancy flier has a ruby throat and looks somewhat like a moth. Although its body is small, it has a very good motor in it, being able to go as fast as sixty times each second. Of course the motor in a hummingbird's body is not made of metal bolts, wheels, and rods. It contains a heart, lungs, and stomach.

Instead of gasoline and oil, the hummingbird's motor uses nectar which the bird sucks from flowers. It needs a good deal of nectar to keep its motor running so fast. Honeysuckles, trumpet vines, phlox, and gladiolas have this sweet liquid buried deep in their blossoms. The hummingbird has a long, sharp beak and a long tongue for sucking its food from these flowers.

The sides of a hummingbird's tongue roll in towards the center, making it into two tubes. The bird runs this two-tube tongue down into the sweet nectar of a flower, drinking it much as boys and girls drink a soda through two straws.

While it hovers over a flower, drinking nectar, it never lights. Its wings, holding it suspended above the flower, go so fast that they can hardly be seen. They make a buzzing sound, louder than a bumble bee. It is the vibration of the wings that makes the sound.

A Ruby-Throat fights an Anna hummingbird that also wants a drink of nectar.

Some insects, also, get their food from flowers but only one, the hawk moth, has as long a tongue as the hummingbird. Besides the nectar in a flower, the hummingbird also sucks up small insects that may have been caught in the nectar.

People who are interested in hummingbirds sometimes put out a special invitation for them to come to their trumpet vines to dine. They wrap tiny bottles in bright colored cloths, fill the bottles with sugar syrup, and tie them to the vines. Any hummingbirds near by are almost sure to accept such a sweet invitation.

The hummingbird also uses its long sharp beak as a weapon. Because there seems to be a great deal of selfishness and bad temper among the members of a hummingbird family, they often use their beaks as weapons. If a member of one hummingbird family should go to one of the favorite flowers of another family, it is usually sent away with some unpleasant pecks.

Although a hummingbird is no longer than your finger, it is brave enough to attack other birds many times as large. A crow, or even a hawk, will retreat in a hurry rather than get into a fight with a hummingbird. It does not have a chance against the noisy little bird that can fly so fast and attack from any angle with its sharp beak.

A hummingbird's nest is hard to see because it is only about as big as an English walnut, and looks like a bump on the limb of a tree. The inside of the nest is shaped like a cup and is not much bigger than a thimble. It is made of fine parts of plants and has a nice soft lining of milkweed or dandelion down. It is fastened to the limb with spider webs, moss, or lichen.

The mother hummingbird lays two small white eggs about the

L. Chace

size of a bean in the nest and then begins sitting on them. Usually the father disappears soon ofter the nest is made. The mother is left alone to sit on the eggs and take all the care of the tiny birds when they hatch. The mother goes off to find food which she swallows and partly digests before giving it to her young ones. When feeding them it looks as if she were stabbing them with her long beak, but she is only putting the food in the babies' throats.

Like many other birds, hummingbirds fly north for the summer months and south for the winter. They build their nests in the northern part of the United States or in the southern part of Canada. They fly south in the fall to the Gulf of Mexico. Some travel to Central America, crossing the Gulf without stopping.

There are many other kinds of hummingbirds besides the ruby-throated hummingbird. Some have blue throats. Others have a streak of black under their beaks. The father bird has the brightest colors, but all hummingbirds have beautiful coloring.

REPTILES

Slippers and Sliders

SNAKES, like lizards, turtles, alligators, and crocodiles, belong to the group of scaly animals called reptiles. But snakes and a few of the lizards are the only reptiles that have no legs.

Snakes seem to go slipping and sliding along the ground. The way they move, however, is more like pushing and pulling themselves along.

The body of a snake is covered with dry scales, and it is not slippery or slimy, as some people think. On the under side of the body the scales are fastened by muscles to the tips of the ribs. A person has twelve pairs of ribs, but a snake may have more than 200.

The scales overlap, one over the other, like the slats in a Venetian blind. The pulling of the muscles raises the free edges of the scales, much as pulling the cord opens the slats of the blind. As the muscles pull on the scales, the edges of the scales push against the ground, moving the snake forward. A snake can move much faster on rough ground than on a smooth surface. If a snake should try to move across a waxed floor, it would have a very bad time of it.

Snakes may move, too, by throwing their bodies into wavelike curves. Some snakes can go so fast that they are called racers, while others climb trees very easily. Still others swim well, and are found so often in water that they are called water snakes.

Bull snakes, sometimes growing nine feet long, are one of the largest kinds to be found in North America. Besides rats, these snakes eat many other kinds of warm-blooded animals, such as mice, gophers, and ground squirrels.

Garter snakes and some other kinds of snakes eat cold-blooded animals such as toads, frogs, and insects. Some snakes, such as the king snake, eat other snakes. Although they sometimes eat poisonous snakes, the poison does not appear to hurt them. Snakes swallow their food whole, and some kinds even swallow it without first killing it.

By pressing against any fixed object at points "P", a snake pushes itself forward with a flowing, weaving motion.

Snake track in sand shows little piles made at points "M" which snake uses as pivots to push body forward.

Others kill by wrapping the coils of their bodies around animals and suffocating them. The huge boa constrictors and anacondas of South America and the pythons of Southeastern Asia kill their victims in this way. Anacondas and pythons are sometimes more than thirty feet long, and one of them can easily kill a full-grown deer or pig. Some snakes kill animals by stabbing them with needle-like hollow teeth to inject poison. Snakes are cold-blooded animals, and do not need as much food as many other animals. The bull snake's dinner of a rat is enough food to last it for a week.

CORN SNAKE

DIAMOND-BACK
RATTLESNAKE

SNAKES FOUND IN
THE UNITED STATES

CORAL SNAKE

KING SNAKE

BULL SNAKE

Snakes are able to swallow animals larger than they are because their upper and lower jaws are held together by elastic-like ligaments, or bands, which stretch to allow the jaws to open wide. The bones of the lower jaws, and in many snakes the bones of both jaws, also, are fastened together at the tip of the mouth by the same kind of bands. When snakes swallow something larger than they are, these bands all stretch to make their mouths much larger.

Once an animal has been caught, there is no chance of its getting away, because the snake holds it firmly in its teeth. The teeth are fine, sharp, and curved so that food cannot slip out of its mouth.

Poisonous snakes have some of the upper teeth connected with poison glands and these teeth are grooved or hollow to carry the poison. When these snakes bite other animals, the poison from the glands runs down into the wounds. In some kinds, there may be only one very large hollow tooth on each side. Such teeth are called poison fangs. Sometimes these fangs are more than half an inch long.

Garter Snake

The only poisonous snakes in the United States are the rattlesnakes, water moccasins, copperheads, and coral snakes. The first three belong to a group called pit vipers. They are distinguished by a hollow or pit on each side between the eye and the nostril.

Rattlesnakes are widely scattered, and some of the different kinds may be found in almost every part of America. The rattle consists of a series of hard dry rings of skin of peculiar shape. As the snake coils to bite, it vibrates its tail, producing a loud buzz. Once a person hears the sharp buzzing sound, he never forgets this strange warning that the snake is getting ready to strike.

The water moccasin is a dark-colored, stout, and ugly looking snake that lives mostly in the swampy parts of southern United States. People often call it the "cottonmouth" moccasin. The inside of its mouth is so white that it looks as if it might be full of cotton. The copperheads are close relatives of the water moccasin.

The common coral snake is found in the southeastern part of the United States. It has a bright coral color trimmed with black and is the most beautiful but also the most poisonous snake in America. There is another small coral snake that lives in the deserts of the southwest. Coral snakes are related to brightly colored poisonous snakes of other parts of the world and to the deadly cobra of India.

If snakes lose any of their teeth, new ones quickly grow in to take the place of the old ones. The fangs are shed quite regularly, and new fangs also grow in to replace the old ones.

Snakes' tongues are long and forked with slender tips. They move rapidly in and out of the snakes' mouths. Snakes use their tongues to feel and touch things, much as people feel with their fingers.

When snakes get too big for their skins they shed them and grow new ones. How often the skin is shed depends upon how fast a snake grows. It may need a new skin several times a year. Even the eyes of snakes are covered with a thin glossy part of the skin. When snakes shed their skins, the eye covering, too, is shed.

Snakes never close their eyes because they do not have eyelids. This makes them seem to stare at everything.

Like many other kinds of snakes, the bull snake lays eggs. A mother bull snake finds a warm, damp place in the ground and lays as many as twenty eggs at one time. Sometimes she crawls into crevices among

Look at the fangs in this head of a diamond-backed rattlesnake.

American Museum of Natural History

Do you see the rattles at the tip of the tail of this rattlesnake?

Field Museum of Natural History

big stones and lays her eggs there. The sun warms the stones and they help to keep the ground and eggs warm.

Each little snake grows about six or eight inches long while it is still inside the egg. A baby snake opens its shell with an "egg tooth" which is a very sharp point on the tip of its snout. Soon after a baby is hatched it loses its egg tooth because it has no more use for it. Baby snakes look like their mothers and are able to take care of themselves as soon as they are hatched. If they should meet their mother they would not know her because she leaves her eggs as soon as they are laid.

A mother rattlesnake does not lay eggs. Her eggs develop inside her body, and the baby snakes are born alive. There may be twelve or more born at one time. The mother rattlesnake does not take care of her babies either, but goes off and leaves them to care for themselves. The common, harmless garter snakes are also born alive.

Most snakes, even the harmless kinds, have good ways of protecting themselves. For instance, many of them cannot be seen easily because of their color. A green grass snake is almost the color of grass. Brown spotted snakes look much like the ground where they live. Some snakes are able to crawl so fast that they can escape enemies in that way, while others slide away into protected places at any sign of danger.

In the autumn, in the colder climates snakes find holes in the ground, or crawl into cracks among the rocks found on the sunny slopes of hills. There they sleep during the winter. This winter sleep is called hibernation. Snakes often gather in large number in such places. Then in the spring when it gets warm, they come out of their sleeping places, stretch and sun themselves, and begin to hunt for food.

The Leatherback Turtle lives in the ocean. This huge turtle may grow to be six feet long and weigh three-quarters of a ton.

Shellbacks of Land and Sea

IF SOMEONE said to you, "Come to see the turtle," you could be sure of at least three things about the animal you were going to see. It would have a shell, a head, and four feet. But you could not be sure of its size, its color, or where it lived.

Some grown turtles are no bigger than a saucer while others may be eight feet long. Some turtles are the color of mud, others are green, and still others look as though parts of them had been covered with bright red or yellow paint.

Some turtles live in water all their lives, while others live entirely on land; but most turtles live partly on land and partly in the water. The turtles that live on land are often called tortoises. Those living in ponds, rivers, and swamps, especially those kinds which are used for food, are often called terrapins, although many people call them "mud turtles." But most people quite properly call all these animals turtles.

A turtle's shell may be rounded like a helmet or flat like a pie pan. The shell is usually made up of a bony box covered with horny scales; but some turtles have only leathery skin over the bone.

The turtles that live in the water have webbed feet to help them swim, but land turtles have no webbing between their toes. All turtles belong to the big group of scaly animals called reptiles.

This is a Green Turtle that lives
in the salt waters along the eastern
coast of the United States. Its
shell is greenish-brown with yellow
markings and it may be 5 feet long
and weigh more than 500 pounds.
While its big front feet make good
flippers for swimming, it cannot
move easily on land. Turtle soup
is often made from its meat.

The upper jaw of this turtle looks
like the hooked bill of a hawk so
it is called the Hawk's-Bill Turtle.
Its shell is covered with thin layers
of yellow and brown horn that gives
us the tortoise shell used to make
combs and many other things.

This pretty little painted terrapin
is often called a Pond Turtle and
is sometimes kept in garden pools as
a pet. Its shell is a greenish color
marked with yellow or red. It rarely
gets larger than five inches across.

This Box Turtle lives on land. It
is usually found in dry woods,
hiding under low, thick bushes.
Its lower shell is divided into
two parts and is held together by
a tough band that forms a hinge.
When danger is near, the box turtle
draws its head, feet, and tail in
between the upper and lower shells.
The shells are then tightly closed,
keeping the turtle safe inside.

The Snapping Turtle is a fresh-
water turtle and lives in
muddy streams, ponds, and lakes.
Most snapping turtles grow
to about twenty-three inches long.

One of the most common and best-known turtles is the snapping turtle. It gets its name from the way it snaps its jaws together. Its head seems to move as fast as lightning, and its jaws snap together so hard that they can take off a man's finger. There are no teeth in the jaw, for no turtles have teeth. Instead the jaw has a horny ridge which is very sharp.

A snapping turtle has a large head and a long tail that looks somewhat like an alligator's tail. Its legs have flabby folds of dirt-colored skin around them, and its feet are webbed. Its rough shell is a dull brown color which makes it hard to be seen when it is in the mud. Sometimes there is green moss growing on a snapping turtle's back, which makes it look like a rock in the edge of the water. The shell may be more than a foot long.

Rivers and lakes are the usual homes for snapping turtles. They swim well, using their webbed feet and tails to paddle through the water. They stick their noses up out of the water to breathe because they have lungs, and would drown if they could not get to the surface for air.

The turtle eggs in this picture are magnified and look much larger than they really are. A mother turtle lays her eggs, then covers them and goes away. After the baby turtles hatch, they make their way to the pond where their mother lives, but they will not know her if they meet her.

This Giant Turtle lives on land. Giant land turtles are found on the Galapagos Islands in the Pacific Ocean. While some weigh as much as 400 pounds, they are not as huge as Leatherback Turtles. Some Giant Turtles live for more than a hundred years.

Snapping turtles seem to swallow only when their heads are under water. They catch and eat many of the smaller animals in the water. Sometimes they catch water birds or small land animals and drag them under water to eat them.

Once a year, about June or July, a mother "snapper" leaves her home at the water's edge to go on land. She finds a soft place in the earth and digs with her back legs until her body is several inches down in the earth. There she lays about twenty-five hard-shelled, round, white eggs. They are only about one-half as large as chicken eggs. After the eggs are laid, she scratches dirt on top of them with her strong hind feet. It takes her several days to lay her eggs and cover them. Then she goes back to the water, for she is tired and hungry and must look for food.

The eggs stay in the hole in the ground for several weeks. When the eggs are ready to hatch, the baby turtles inside break the shells with their egg teeth. They push and twist and turn until their heads are out. Next they get their front feet out. It is hard work for a turtle to get out of its shell. Sometimes it takes several hours.

After the baby turtles are hatched, they make their way to the water. There they swim about and look for food just as grown turtles do. Soon they lose their egg teeth.

Snapping turtles hibernate during the winter. As the water gets colder and colder, the turtles go down deeper and deeper into the mud at the bottom of the pond. They lie quietly until spring comes.

One kind of snapping turtle is huge. It is the Alligator Snapping Turtle and it is the largest North American land or fresh-water turtle. It is also called a Luggerhead turtle and is found in the Mississippi River and other rivers in the southern part of our country.

Alligator

Crocodile

Crocodile   Alligator
Comparison
of Heads

Giant Reptiles

THE CHINESE and Japanese people often use pictures of the dragon for decoration, and many of their folk tales and fairy stories are about this make-believe monster. Perhaps the alligators found in China today, or the crocodiles in Africa, are responsible for the stories about monsters that breathed fire.

Alligators and crocodiles are the biggest living reptiles. Some alligators grow to be about fifteen feet long, and crocodiles grow even longer. Except for some sharks, crocodiles are the largest animals that hatch from eggs.

Like most other reptiles, alligators and crocodiles are covered with scales. The scales on their backs are very hard and bony, but the covering on the other parts of their bodies is more like leather. The leathery part of their skins is used to make shoes, purses, and belts, and even the bony back is sometimes used.

These two reptiles look much alike, but the nose of most crocodiles is quite pointed, while an alligator's head is more blunt and rounded. Crocodiles are more ferocious than alligators. Their teeth are larger than alligators' teeth. Even when a crocodile closes its mouth some of its big teeth may be seen. An alligator's teeth almost never show when its mouth is closed.

Look at the alligator and the crocodile in the picture on the facing page. In what ways are they alike? Do you see one important way in which they are different? The crocodile has a narrow head and a pointed snout. The alligator has a broad head and a round snout.

Both these giant reptiles have huge mouths and powerful jaws. They can strike terrific blows with their long, thick tails, and do not hesitate to attack large animals such as deer or cattle. The victim may be stunned by one blow from the giant reptile's tail or it may be seized in its jaws, before being dragged under water by the monster.

When on land, crocodiles and alligators usually stay away from people. But in the water they are able to move about more easily. Many natives have lost their lives while swimming in the warm rivers of Africa because they were seized by crocodiles. For this reason some crocodiles in Africa are called man-eaters, and people say that these animals have even attacked small boats.

Both of these types of giant reptiles have a row of sharp teeth on each side of each jaw which shows plainly when they open their mouths.

Florida State News Bureau

Once there were many wild alligators, but so many were killed for sport or for their hides that today there are laws to protect them from hunters. There are alligator farms, too, where alligators are raised. This picture shows the St. Augustine Alligator Farm in Florida.

The teeth, like those of other reptiles, are often lost. Each tooth is shaped somewhat like an ice cream cone with the point of a new tooth growing up inside the old one. When the old tooth comes out, a new one is there to take its place.

Alligators and crocodiles also have strange tongues. Our tongues

Acme

Do you see the strong jaws and sharp teeth in this alligator's head?

are fastened at the back, and a toad's tongue is fastened at the front. But the under side of the tongues of these reptiles is fastened to their lower jaws all the way around. Their tongues are so thick, however, that they can be raised and lowered even if they are fastened underneath.

When these reptiles are under water they can raise a fleshy valve at the back of the mouth to close up their throats. Then they can open their big mouths as wide as they need to, and no water runs down their throats.

Both of these reptiles swim well, but they do not use their feet in swimming. They hold their feet close to their bodies to make themselves more streamlined. Then they push through the water by flipping their big tails from side to side. Often they float near the surface with only their eyes and ears and noses above the water. Their ears are just behind their eyes. A bony flap that can be opened and closed grows over each ear. This flap is kept closed while they are in the water.

Mother alligators and mother crocodiles both leave the water and crawl out on land to lay their eggs. Either one of these mothers may dig a hole in the sand to lay her eggs or she may build a mound for them out of twigs, leaves, and moss. The eggs are white and have hard shells. About two or three dozen eggs are laid, usually in several layers, one on top of another. Between the layers, the mother reptile places mud and grass and leaves, then she covers them carefully with more grass and leaves. As soon as the eggs are laid, the mother goes back to the water.

The sun and the rotting grass and leaves keep the eggs warm until they hatch. Little alligators are black with yellow markings, and crocodile babies are greenish brown with black markings. As the babies grow up, they lose their markings.

These baby reptiles eat fish and other animals that live in the water. The parents eat fish too, but they also catch land animals that go to the water's edge to get a drink.

Alligators and crocodiles both live in warm climates. The American alligator is found in the southeastern part of the United States, living mostly in rivers and swamps. The only kind of crocodile in North America is found in some wild swamp land near the coast of the southern tip of Florida, but there are many others living in the warm rivers of South America, Africa, and Asia.

Alligators can stand more cold than crocodiles, so they live a little farther north than crocodiles do. The only other true alligator besides our own lives in China. Alligators, like turtles and frogs, spend the winter buried in the mud.

AMPHIBIANS

From Swimmers to Jumpers

ONE SPRING day a little frog tadpole, no bigger than a mosquito, twisted and turned until it worked its way out of a mass of jelly which held many black and white eggs together. It had no eyes, ears, legs, or mouth. But it had a tail, and in the place of a mouth, it had a sucker. With the sucker, it held onto the jelly from which it had hatched because it was too helpless to swim.

By the end of the second or third day, the little tadpole had changed a great deal. It was able to swim by flipping its tail. It could take air out of the water because it had grown little gills, which looked like fringes on each side of its head. Instead of a sucker, it had a mouth with sharp lips with which it could scrape up tiny green plants to eat. By this time the tadpole also had eyes.

As the tadpole ate plants and grew a fold of skin began to grow over the fringed gills. Now they were inside the tadpole's head. It took water into its mouth to get oxygen, and the water passed over the gills and out of a small opening on the left side of its body.

During the next weeks, the tadpole kept on growing and changing. In place of gills, lungs were growing. Without gills, the tadpole could not breathe in water. It swam to the top of the water to get air into its lungs.

Close to the tail, two small legs appeared. In a few more days, when the hind legs had

grown large, there was a front foot where the little hole on the left side of its body had been. Then a small bump appeared on the right side of its body and this also burst out as another tiny front foot and leg. By this time, the tadpole could climb among the plants in the pond and could even go out on land for a few minutes at a time; and its tail kept getting shorter and shorter.

The tadpole's eyes were beginning to bulge, its mouth was getting big, and it was growing a tongue. Soon it would be able to eat grasshoppers and worms just as its father and mother had done. Meanwhile it used up the food stored in its tail.

Then, one day there was no tail at all—and there was no tadpole—because the little tadpole had become a frog. It was sitting on the edge of the pond keeping a sharp watch for insects. It had a sticky tongue and a big mouth.

Its tongue was fastened at the front of its mouth, instead of the back as yours is. Your tongue points out of your mouth, but a frog's tongue points down its throat. When an insect flies near the mouth of a frog, the long sticky tongue flips out, full length. The insect is almost sure to stick to the tip of the tongue.

This little frog ate a great deal and grew so big that its skin became too small. When this happened the frog just pulled off the old skin, and there underneath was a new one to take its place. As soon as the old skin was shed, it was sucked into the frog's mouth and eaten. The frog continued to grow so rapidly that it had to shed its skin several times before it really grew up.

Any animal must eat a great deal of food to grow fast and at the same time store up enough to last it through the winter. The frog ate many insects and worms. Then, like other grown-up frogs, it hibernated. It found a soft, muddy place in the edge of the pond where the water was not deep. There it wiggled its way down into the mud and went to sleep. While it slept, it breathed through its skin and used the stored-up food in its body.

After a winter in hibernation, the frog came out from the mud at the edge of the pond. It was very hungry, but before it could look for food it needed to find a male frog for a mate. There were many male frogs croaking loudly near the pond, and they all seemed to be calling for mates. This frog found one and both frogs leaped into the pond. They chose a hidden place in the shallow water, and there the female frog laid several thousand eggs and the male fertilized them. The male and female frogs then went in search of food because they were both thin and hungry after sleeping all winter.

Not all the eggs hatched because some were eaten by hungry fishes. Many tadpoles that hatched were also eaten, but some became frogs.

Leopard frogs are grayish-green with black spots edged with white. These frogs get their name from being spotted like a leopard. Leopard frogs spend much of their time out in the green grass where there are plenty of flies, bugs, and grasshoppers to eat. Because of their green color, they blend into the green of the grass. This helps protect them from enemies.

Their green color helps frogs live safely. They also have other ways of protecting themselves.

Leopard Frog

97

This young bullfrog croaks by forcing air back and forth past his vocal chords. That is how all frogs make sounds.

Century

A grown-up leopard frog is only about four inches long, but it can jump fifteen times that far. It can puff itself up until it is plump, at the same time moistening its skin until it becomes slick. A jumping frog that is slick and plump is not easy to catch or hold. You can see how hard it is for a frog's enemies—snakes, turtles, and water birds—to catch a frog.

Bullfrogs are the largest frogs in the United States, sometimes being as much as eight inches long. They are greenish-brown in color and have yellow throats. In the northern states their babies stay in the tadpole stage for more than two years and grow to be several inches long before they change into frogs. In the winter, the bullfrog tadpoles hibernate in the soft mud at the bottom of the pond just as grown-up bullfrogs do.

There are several kinds of small frogs called "tree frogs." Some of them change their color to brown, gray, or green, depending upon the color of the trees or plants they are sitting on. Changing color is a great protection, because if one of these little frogs is among green leaves, by changing to green it cannot be seen easily; if it is on a gray twig, it turns gray.

It is easy for tree frogs to climb trees and even to walk on smooth surfaces because their toes have little pads that help them stick. Tree frogs do most of their moving about in the evening. They jump from one tree branch to another, catching insects with their sticky tongues. They also do most of their croaking, or singing, in the evening, or often when the air grows moist before a rain.

Do you know how to tell a
grown-up frog and toad apart?
Look at the rough, warty gray
skin of this toad. A frog's
skin is smooth, moist, and shiny.

Philip Gendreau

Toads are like frogs in many ways. Both of them are cold-blooded and are called amphibians because they spend part of their lives in water and the rest on land. Neither one has tails and their bodies are short and stubby. The front legs are short and used for balancing, and to keep them from falling forward on their faces. The long, stout back legs are useful for jumping and swimming, and most surprisingly, for digging themselves down into the ground backward.

Frogs and toads can see in almost every direction. Their eyes which look like dark, shiny beads, seem to be popping out of their heads. When their eyes close, one pair of eyelids moves up from the bottom and another down from the top. The top eyelids are so small and tight they push the eyes of the toads and frogs down into their heads. Then their eyes cannot be injured easily.

Toads and frogs have what we would consider bad eating manners because they swallow their food whole. Sometimes they catch such big worms that the front feet are used as pushers to help cram the worms into their mouths. Frogs have a row of tiny teeth in the upper jaw but toads have no teeth at all.

All tadpoles are hatched from tiny black and white eggs laid in ponds. Toads' eggs, held together in strings of jelly, look almost like strings of beads. Frogs' eggs, each in a tiny jelly ball, usually form masses or balls of jelly. The jelly protects the eggs.

Toad tadpoles are black and change into toads when they are very small, while frog tadpoles are brown or some other color and grow to a much larger size before their legs appear.

FISHES

Fishes from Green to Gold

YEARS ago there were no goldfish, but there were many small green fish swimming wild in the rivers of China and Japan. Nobody paid much attention to these dull green fish until one day some Chinese noticed that one of the fish had spots of gold color on it.

The fish was caught and given especially good care. Many people in China became interested in it, and looked for a mate for it that also had a little gold color. When the eggs were laid, they, too, were carefully watched.

Several of the young fish that hatched from these eggs had some gold color. Those that had the most gold on them were placed with mates that showed some gold. When more eggs were laid and the grandchildren of the first gold-spotted green fish hatched, they had more gold than either their parents or grandparents.

By carefully selecting the young fish and their mates, the Chinese finally had many fish that were all-gold colored. Besides, they found that they were able to raise fish of other colors from the small wild ones.

All the fish that were raised in this way were called goldfish, although some of them were silver, black, or spotted. Goldfish with odd eyes and tails were developed, also, by the plan of careful selection. Now fancy goldfish are raised in many parts of the world.

Like other fishes, goldfish never close their eyes, because they have no eyelids. A fish does not need eyelids. Its eyes are kept clean and moist by the water in which it lives. A fish cannot see well when it is taken out of the water.

Although fish cannot hear as well as people, sound waves are carried through the water and reach their ears, which are inside their bodies. Fish, also, have a good sense of smell.

A goldfish has seven fins, each of which helps it to swim. The tail is the paddle or propeller. As it flips back and forth pushing against the water, it makes the fish move forward. The back fin and the single fin on the under side of the body are the steering fins. They guide the fish through the water. The fish's "arm and leg fins" on its sides are called paired fins. They help the fish to keep its balance and, also, are used as emergency brakes.

The scales on a fish's body overlap like the shingles on a roof. Placed with their edges toward the back, they do not catch the water as the fish moves ahead. Thus the scales protect its body without hindering the fish in any of its movements.

Fish seem to swallow water when they breathe. As the gill covers on the sides of a fish's head open and close, water is taken into the fish's mouth, but it is not swallowed. When it passes back over the gills and out under the gill covers, the gills take oxygen from it.

Like most kinds of fish, the mothers lay eggs. But usually they pay no attention to the eggs, or to the young after they are hatched.

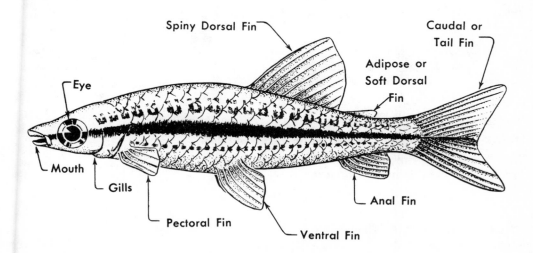

The body of a fish is streamlined to cut through the water easily.

Harry Goodman from Shostal

These colorful fish live in the fresh waters of the tropics. They are
often found in aquariums because of their bright, beautiful colors.
This picture was taken in an aquarium. Do you know how you can tell?
Coral does not belong to fresh waters. It is found only in salt waters.

1. Red Platy 2. Tiger Barb 3. Giant Danio 4. Red Wagtail
5. Sunset Platy 6. Pencilfish 7. Paradise Fish 8. Black Molly
9. Black Angel 10. Kissing Gourami 11. Betta 12. Serpae
13. Red Swordtail 14. Coral

A King Among Fishes

IT WAS early spring and the sun shone down on the calm Pacific Ocean. Under the surface of the water there was a flash of silver as a big Pacific salmon opened its mouth and devoured a smaller fish. about a foot long. The big salmon was about five feet long and weighed about 100 pounds.

This huge fish, sometimes called Chinook or king salmon, was getting ready to make a long trip up the Columbia River where the salmon eggs would be laid and fertilized. Other Pacific salmon were preparing to make the trip, too, but only a few were as large as this one. Most of them weighed about twenty-five pounds.

These salmon had lived in the Pacific Ocean for several years while they grew up. Now they were ready to leave the salt water of the ocean, never to return. For the few days remaining they rested and ate a great many fish. Once they were on their way they would do no more eating.

At last, it was time for them to go. Great numbers of the shiny, silver-colored fish swam out of the ocean and started up the river. The big migration trip, called a salmon "run," had begun. The fish seemed so eager to get up the river that they bumped into each other and sometimes piled up. Hundreds of them splashed in the water and leaped into the air.

The water was not salty as it had been in the ocean, and the fish had to swim against the current as they moved up the river. In a few days they all lost their beautiful silver color and turned to a dirty

103

brown. On and on they swam without stopping for food. The fat that they had stored up while they were in the Pacific kept them alive.

Sometimes the swimming was not hard. Then the fish could make as much as four miles in a day. At other times they swam into such swift currents that they seemed to be pushed backward faster than they could go ahead. Then, perhaps, they would swim into swift whirlpools that took them around and around. But whatever happened each day they managed to get a little farther up the river.

At Bonneville, about a hundred miles from the Pacific, the fish came to a huge, concrete dam across the Columbia River. There they found fish ladders to help them on their way. They also found elevators, or locks filled with water, in which the fish were lifted past the dam to a higher level. The United States Government built these ladders and locks to help the Pacific salmon continue on their important trip up the river.

Oregon State Highway Department Photo

These fish ladders at Bonneville Dam, Oregon, help the salmon make their way up the river. Each ladder step is a foot high. The fish jump up to a step and then rest in a pool before they make the next leap.

Some of the king salmon became too tired to complete the trip, but they swam on until they died. One day some of them reached the bottom of some waterfalls where it seemed impossible that they could go on. But there also, they jumped flopping as high as six feet in order to get over the falls. Many of the fish were knocked against sharp rocks and were cut and bruised, and some were killed. But the remaining salmon kept on trying until they either jumped the falls or died in the attempt.

American Museum of Natural History

This salmon is leaping over a falls.

For days and weeks many of the fish swam on. Some, after traveling several hundred miles, turned into small branches or tributaries of the river. Others went as far as a thousand miles or more up the Columbia River. One of the strange things about the migration of the salmon is that each fish finds its way back to the place where it was hatched several years before.

The salmon were all thin and hungry when they reached their destinations. But as soon as they arrived, the mother fish began looking for places to lay their eggs. Each found a place in the river where there was a gravel bottom and the water was not deep or flowing too fast.

There, using her head and tail, she hollowed out a place in the gravel, sometimes called a nest. In this hollow place she laid several hundred pink eggs that looked like jewels about the size of peas. The father fish swam close beside the mother leaving a milky liquid called milt over the eggs as they were laid. Without the milt to fertilize them, they would not hatch. Each mother fish made nest after nest until her several thousand eggs were laid and fertilized. Each nest was dug a little farther up the river than the last one so that the gravel that was thrown up in digging the next nest drifted gently back to cover the new-laid eggs and make them safe. When fish lay and fertilize their eggs, the process is called *spawning*.

Salmon do not look after their eggs or the baby fish that are hatched from them. So, as soon as the eggs were spawned, the big fish left and began their return trip down the Columbia River towards the Pacific Ocean. They were so tired after their long trip without food, and their spawning of thousands of eggs, that they let the current carry them back down the river. Usually they just floated, tails first, downstream. Within a few hours most of them died, and none of them lived to reach the ocean again.

Some of the salmon eggs hatched in about two months, but many of them were eaten by other animals of the river. Many of the little fish that hatched had no chance to grow up because they were eaten by other fishes. But there were perhaps several hundred baby salmon left from each fish's spawning.

The baby fish soon started swimming around but they did not need to look for food at first. The yolk of the egg from which it had hatched hung on the underside of each little fish's body, and furnished it with food. When the yolk was gone the fish started to look for other foods. They gathered tiny bits of plant and animal matter that were floating in the water.

When the little fish were two or three inches long most of them began to swim off downstream. The river was flowing so fast that they found it easy swimming. They were carried over the falls and along with the current, and, in a short time, were out in the big Pacific Ocean where their mothers and fathers had been.

The fish you see in this picture are some of the most popular fresh-water game fish. Fishermen enjoy the thrill of battling these fish for they fight long and fiercely for their freedom when they are hooked.

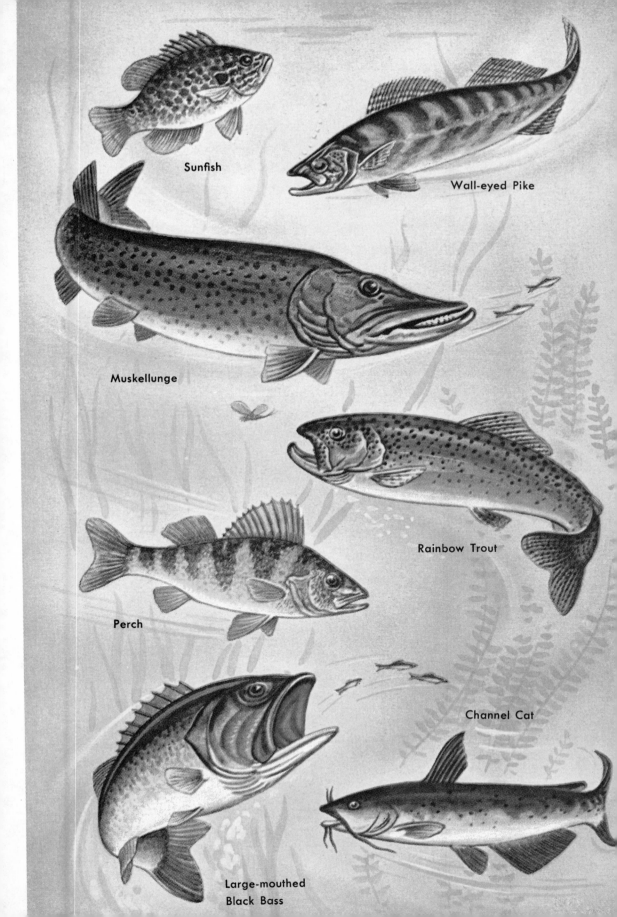

Sunfish

Wall-eyed Pike

Muskellunge

Rainbow Trout

Perch

Channel Cat

Large-mouthed
Black Bass

For several years the young salmon swam around in the ocean. They followed schools of other kinds of fish through the water and ate many of the smaller ones. The more they ate, the faster they grew, and the fatter they became. After several years they were as big as their parents had been. Then they, too, began their adventurous trip up the Columbia River.

What drives each generation of salmon to make the dangerous journey to the spawning grounds? We do not know, but we do know that there are many kinds of fishes and they differ in many ways. Some fish, like the sunfish and the rainbow trout, are brilliantly colored. Others are dull and drab in color. Some fish are long and slender. Others are short and stubby.

Some kinds of fish, like the muskellunge, are a terror to other fishes, for they eat only smaller fishes and other animals. Other fish eat only plants, while still others eat both animals and plants.

Some fish live only in cold waters, others only in warm waters. Some kinds live only in lakes and rivers. Other fish are found only in a particular part of an ocean.

As scientists study fish and their habits, they learn more and more about them.

Men have been learning about fish ever since a cave man first speared a fish for food. Today we still fish for food and for fun. It is an exciting thrill when a game fish snaps at your bait and you proudly reel him in!

INSECTS

A Monarch Butterfly

ONE DAY a beautiful monarch butterfly flew over a milkweed plant growing beside the road. The plant had soft green leaves and its flowers were bright orange —the same color as the butterfly. In a moment the butterfly fluttered down to the plant and then laid several eggs on the under side of one of the leaves. While she was on the plant it was hard to see her because she looked so much like one of the plant's flowers.

After several days the eggs hatched into black and white larvae no bigger than a small letter "i" on this page. These were not worms although some people might call them that. They were tiny caterpillars.

The caterpillars moved about on the milkweed plant and ate the leaves. They ate almost all the time, both day and night. They grew fast and soon were too big for their skins; so they grew new skins and crawled out of their old ones. This is called *molting*.

The caterpillars molted several times. After about two weeks of molting they were almost as big as your little finger, and had turned into large green, yellow, and orange striped caterpillars.

One of them crawled out under a leaf of the milkweed plant where it spun a pad of silk and fastened itself to the pad. Hanging with its head down, the caterpillar molted once more. This time, instead of getting a new skin it got a green bag with gold and black trim-

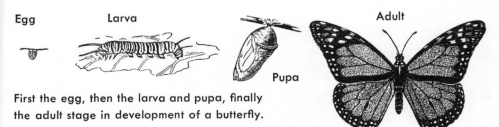

Egg   Larva   Pupa   Adult

First the egg, then the larva and pupa, finally the adult stage in development of a butterfly.

109

ming, sometimes called the monarch's "green house with gold nails."

The other caterpillars found other milkweed leaves on which to molt. Some of them, however, may have crawled out on a fence wire or dead twig to make their new homes.

While it was in its green bag, the monarch butterfly was going through what is called the *pupa* stage. The green bag with the caterpillar inside was a *chrysalis*. It was about the size and shape of a candy bean, but much more beautiful. The pupa stage is often called the resting stage, although this is not a good name because many changes go on inside the chrysalis.

One day the green bag turned a bluish black and began to move. Two feet came out of the bag, two more feet, and finally there was an orange-brown butterfly with six feet and four wings. The four wings looked wet and crumpled. But the butterfly began to fan them up and down and soon they were large and beautiful. The tiny caterpillar had at last become a full grown insect known as the monarch butterfly.

In the north, adult monarch butterflies often migrate, although most of their relatives do not. In the fall hundreds of these bright insects may gather together to start their trip south. Trees have been seen so full of monarch butterflies that at first they looked as though they were full of orange-colored flowers. Early in the spring these butterflies fly north again. Scientists do not know how they find their way from one part of the country to another.

Butterflies' wings look as though they were covered with powder. But when placed under a microscope, that which looks like powder is really many tiny scales. These scales, which give the wings their colors, are arranged in an orderly way. Because they have scales on their wings butterflies belong to a group of insects that are called *scale wings*.

Monarch butterflies have long, thin, tubelike tongues with which they suck nectar from flowers. They also have feelers with knobs on the ends.

Although usually not eaten by birds, grown butterflies have other enemies such as lizards, wasps, beetles, and certain mammals. Monarch butterflies do little harm and much good. Like the bees, they spread pollen from flower to flower. Some of their relatives, however, are very destructive of certain trees and important farm crops because the growing larvae eat so many of the leaves.

Opposite: Some Common Insects

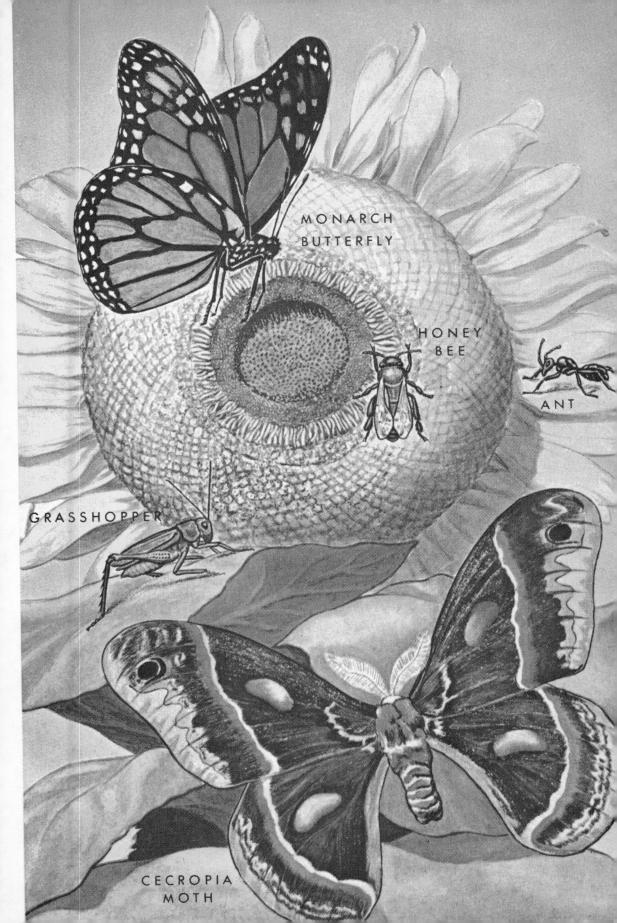

MONARCH
BUTTERFLY

HONEY
BEE

ANT

GRASSHOPPER

CECROPIA
MOTH

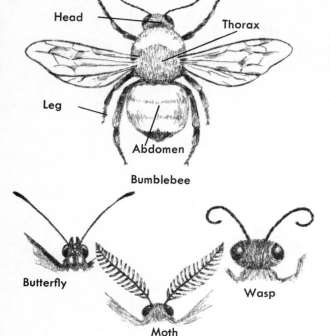

Head
Thorax
Leg
Abdomen
Bumblebee

Butterfly
Wasp
Moth

This Is an Insect

Every insect has three parts to its body. These are the head, the thorax, and the abdomen. Every insect has six legs.

Every insect has two feelers, or *antennae*, on its head. Wasps and ants also use their antennae to taste. Different kinds of insects have different kinds of antennae.

Most insects have one large eye on each side of the head. This eye is made up of many tiny lenses and is called a *compound* eye. Some insects, such as the grasshopper, have both a compound eye and an eye with one lens, or *simple* eye.

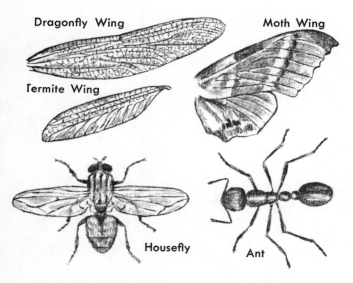

Dragonfly Wing
Moth Wing
Termite Wing

Housefly
Ant

Most insects have two pairs of wings attached to the thorax. Different kinds of insects have different kinds of wings.

Some insects, such as the fly, have only one pair of wings. Some insects, such as the worker ant, have no wings.

Some insects spoil food or carry disease germs. Some eat field or garden crops. But insects help us much more than they harm us. One of the most important ways in which insects help us is by carrying pollen from one plant to another. This helps the plants produce seeds. It helps more and more plants to grow. We need plants to provide food for the world.

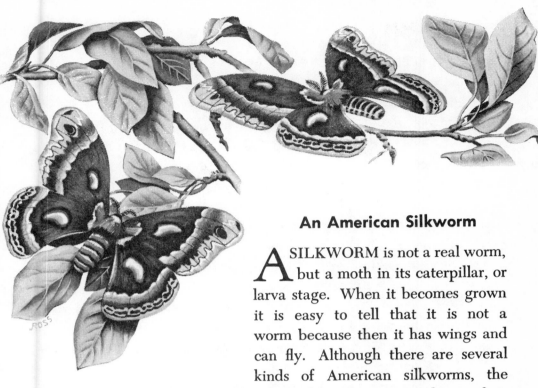

An American Silkworm

A SILKWORM is not a real worm, but a moth in its caterpillar, or larva stage. When it becomes grown it is easy to tell that it is not a worm because then it has wings and can fly. Although there are several kinds of American silkworms, the *cecropia* moth is one of the largest. When it is grown, this moth is often five inches from the edge of one wing to the edge of the other. It is about twice as large as the monarch butterfly.

Like the monarch butterfly, the cecropia moth is an insect which goes through four stages during its life—the egg, larva, pupa, and adult stages. Most people think of the caterpillar, or larva stage, when they call these moths silkworms.

One spring day two beautiful cecropia moths were found in a plum tree. They were very quiet because moths do most of their flying at night. The next day the two moths were gone, but about thirty little cream colored eggs had been left on a leaf. They were the shape and size of large pinheads and they were glued fast to the leaf.

Soon the eggs hatched into baby caterpillars. The caterpillars were black at first and not quite a quarter of an inch long. They seemed very hungry and began at once to eat the leaf on which they had hatched. Soon they moved to other leaves which they also ate. These caterpillars, or larvae, had such big appetites that they ate almost all day long and all night, too.

It happened that a girl passed the plum tree where the caterpillars   **113** were eating and saw them. She broke off the branch of the tree which they were on and put it in a jar of water on her screened back porch. Each day she put a fresh plum branch in the jar of water to give the caterpillars more leaves to eat.

About four days later, the caterpillars become too big for their skins. Their skins split open and fell off, leaving them in soft new suits. The caterpillars were then a brownish-orange color, but there were many little black warty bumps on their bodies. In about six more days, the caterpillars' skins again were too small so they shed them. The next suits were yellow and many of the warty bumps were greenish-blue or orange-red.

The third time they changed suits, or molted, the caterpillars became bluish-green with yellow, orange, and blue warty bumps. When they molted for the fourth time, they did not change color. By this time they had grown to be more than three inches long and bigger around than your finger. They were at least a dozen times as large as they were when they first hatched.

During all of this larva stage, the caterpillars stayed on the plum branches and ate leaves. Then, about two weeks after they had molted for the fourth time, one of the caterpillars crawled down the plum branch, across the floor and up the leg of a chair. There, under the seat, it made its *cocoon* by winding a long silk thread around its body. At last the caterpillar was completely covered with silk.

The silk thread came from the caterpillars's mouth and was made inside its own body.

One of the other caterpillars crawled up over the door to wrap itself in silk, and another crawled to the corner of the porch.

Their cocoons were like hammocks, closed in on all sides and at both ends. On the outside they looked much like brown paper. While the moths were in their cocoons they were in the pupa stage.

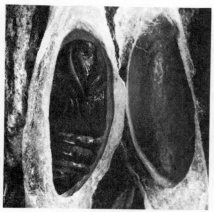

L. Chace

Opened cocoon shows pupa stage.

All winter long the cocoons stayed on the porch. In the spring a moth, wet and crumpled, crawled out of each of the cocoons. Each moth had six feet with which it clung to the porch as it fanned its four crumpled wings up and down. In a few hours each had become a beautiful cecropia moth.

When the girl saw the moths she opened the porch door and let them fly away. They went in search of a place to lay their eggs. They did not eat food but lived on what they had stored up while they were larvae. A few days after they laid their eggs, they died.

If this had been in China, the girl who took care of the silkworms probably would have used the silk soon after the cocoons were formed, for it is from these threads that silk cloth is made. American silkworms make silk much like those in China do, although they are not raised for that purpose. The silk of the cecropia moth is even stronger than that of the Chinese silkworm cocoon.

Like monarch butterflies, cecropia moths belong to the group of insects called scale wings. However, moths and butterflies are different in some ways. The bodies of moths usually are larger and not as slender as those of butterflies. Most moths have feelers which look like feathers instead of the straight feelers with knobs on the ends that butterflies have. They do most of their flying at night while butterflies fly in the daytime. When butterflies light they hold their wings straight up over their backs. Most moths hold their wings spread out open or directed backward along their sides.

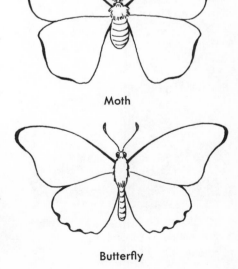

Moth

Butterfly

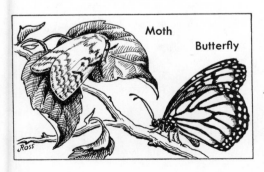

Moth

Butterfly

A cross section of an underground ant colony.

An Insect Community

CAN you imagine a town or city of insects working busily together? A colony of ants does just this. Ants are called *social insects* because they live and work together in groups as people do.

There are thousands of different kinds of ants in the world, but probably the black ant is the most common for it is found in almost all countries north of the Equator.

The next time you see a hole in the ground with a mound of earth around it, stop and look carefully. The hole may be the front door of a black ant colony, for these ants build their homes, or *nests*, under the ground.

The hole leads down to a tunnel that branches off in many directions, making a network of tunnels. There may be several outside doors or openings into the tunnels. At various spots, the tunnels widen to make rooms.

Some rooms are ant nurseries where ant eggs, ant larvae, and ant pupae are tended by worker ant nurses. Other rooms are storerooms for food or "barns" where ant cows, or *aphids*, are kept.

There are usually three classes of ants in a colony—queen ants, male ants, and worker ants.

Worker Ant

Male Ant

Queen Ant

A queen lays eggs.

Eggs

A nurse ant feeds larvae.

Pupa

How does an ant colony begin? It is started by a queen. Queens and male ants are born with thin wings that are somewhat like those of a bee. As soon as a young queen is strong enough, she flies away from her home. A young male flies with her, and they mate in the air. This is the only flight the ants make because soon after they land, the male dies and the queen tears off her own wings.

Then the queen digs a small tunnel under a stone or clump of roots. At the end of the tunnel, she builds a room. When it is finished, she closes its opening. It may take several days of hard work to make the room, and the queen becomes very tired.

For a little while she rests. Then she begins to lay tiny, oval-shaped eggs. After a few days, the eggs hatch into larvae which the queen feeds with a liquid from her body. The larvae grow slowly and spin cocoons around themselves. Now the baby ants are in the pupa stage. They stay in their cocoons until they are full-grown ants.

The first ants that are born are all worker ants. As soon as they break out of their cocoons, they open the front door and go out to find food and bring it back to the queen. She has not eaten since leaving her old home and is weak and hungry.

Then the worker ants begin to dig more tunnels and make more rooms. The queen does not help them. She may live for several more years but her only work is to lay eggs. She does not feed or care for the babies. The worker nurse ants do that.

See the ant breaking out of its cocoon.

The nurses are very particular about the care of the babies of the colony. The tiny eggs are sticky on the outside. The nurses shape them into small balls by sticking many of them together. The egg balls are easy for the nurses to carry about in their jaws from room to room.

The nurses see that the eggs are kept warm so that they will hatch. If one room seems too cold, they carry them to a warmer one. In the daytime while the sun shines, they usually take the eggs to an upper room but at night after those rooms lose the sun's warmth, they carry the egg balls to a lower room. As soon as the eggs are hatched, the tiny larvae are fed a fluid from the nurses' bodies.

After the larvae have been fed several times they make cocoons and pass into the pupa stage. The largest cocoons hold the queens. The workers carry the cocoons from room to room as they did the eggs. Sometimes they are carried up and placed under a stone or board where it is warm. If the stone or board happens to be lifted the workers quickly grab the pupae and hurry to another place. The ants will not go off and leave the pupae because in the ant family the babies are always protected as much as possible.

Even after the pupae are full-grown ants, the workers still protect and feed them until they are strong enough to look after themselves. For a time their legs and bodies are limp and they are weak and helpless. During this time they are called *callows*. As soon as they become strong, the young queens and males make their flight into the air, for they have wings. The workers, which have no wings, begin their duties in the old home—tunneling out new rooms, nursing, housekeeping, or carrying food to the ant kitchen.

The worker ants do well in finding food even though they cannot see well. They can both feel and smell with their feelers, or *antennae*. As the workers run busily back and forth getting food for the colony, they often stop to touch the feelers of other ants, just as though they might be exchanging a message. Sometimes they bring back foods, such as large seeds, that are bigger than they are. Then other workers help them drag the food inside.

The black ant colony not only lives on the solid foods which the workers bring in, but they also keep "cows" which furnish them with a plant liquid called honeydew. Their cows are plant lice, or aphids, which live on the roots, stems, or leaves of plants. When they stroke the aphids with their antennae, these queer cows give the ants drops of the honeydew.

During the winter the ants carefully hide many of the aphids in an underground room. The aphids are carried in the ants' powerful jaws, just as the eggs, larvae, pupae, and callows are carried. In the spring

This ant is stroking an aphid, or ant cow, with its antennae.

the ants carry their cows back to tender green plants so that they will be sure to have a fresh supply of honeydew.

The black ant colony keeps on getting larger. Sometimes soldier ants come to rob the nest of its pupae. The black ant workers try to carry their pupae to safety but there may be so many soldiers that many of the black ants are killed and most of the pupae stolen. After the enemy ants leave, the workers that are left put the home in order again and go on with their duties. The pupae which are carried away are either eaten for food or raised to be slaves in the enemy ant home. This explains why black ants are sometimes found working in a nest of red ants.

Sometimes the ants have a queer guest in their colony. It is a beetle which walks about among the ants begging liquid food. The ants appear to be very good hosts, serving food to the beetle every time it comes near. Then one day the beetle may leave, never to come back. If it stays on, as beetles often do, the ants may run short of food for the baby ants.

An ant colony may live for many years in the same place. As it grows, it enlarges its home. The mound of dirt by the door keeps getting higher as the ants make their tunnels deeper. If the ant home is in someone's yard, it may spoil a section of the lawn. Also the ants' cows suck the juice of the new, green leaves on nearby plants making them shrivel up and fall off. Some of the ants may find their way into the homes of people nearby.

When ants thus become pests people usually try to get rid of the colony. Sometimes the ant home may be almost destroyed but it is hard to get rid of all the thousands of ants living there. A few ants always seem to be saved. They take up their duties again and in a few months, more ants are busily at work.

Wherever people go in the world, they are almost sure to find ants. Among the thousands of kinds are these: the yellow ant which steals sugar from kitchens; the tailor ant which uses the silk-like thread from ant babies' cocoons to mend its home; and the leaf-cutting ant which strips the leaves from trees. To keep the leaves from dragging on the ground as they carry them back to their nests, the leaf-cutting ants hold them over their heads like parasols. This is the reason why people sometimes call them "parasol ants". Later they chew up the leaves and use them to fertilize mushroom or fungus gardens which are raised in special rooms. The leaf-cutting ants use only these mushrooms for food.

The Australian bulldog ant is one of the biggest kinds and is a hard fighter. The carpenter ant burrows its way into logs or partially rotted wood. White ants, or termites, are insects which eat their way through the wooden parts of houses, making them unsafe, but they are relatives of cockroaches and are not real ants.

Then there are the army ants which will attack any animal that they can catch. These warlike ants line up in a military formation and march along eating almost everything on their way. They have no homes but make themselves at home wherever they are. Such an army of ants carries its queen and babies with it. Sometimes the whole army gathers in a ball with the queen and babies protected in the center. The ball may be big enough to fill a bushel basket.

When army ants are on the march, even large animals are not safe if these insects begin to eat the animal's flesh. In Africa and South America, where these ants live, they have been known to clear small villages of almost every living thing. Even an elephant or an anteater is not brave enough to face such an army.

Worker

Queen

Drone

A Family of Honeybees

A HONEYBEE FAMILY usually consists of several thousand bees, and there may be as many as 50,000. In all of these there is one mother, or queen bee, and perhaps about 100 males or drones. The rest are worker bees.

Like other insects, honeybees have six legs and three body parts. They have two pairs of strong wings and five eyes, two of which are compound, or made up of many eyes. To grow up, bees go through the four stages which many insects do—egg, larva, pupa, and adult.

The queen, drones, and workers do not look alike. The queen has a long, pointed body. All she does is to lay eggs in the comb cells which the workers have prepared. Her long, pointed body enables her to place the eggs deep in the cells.

The drones are large and plump. Although they do not work, they are very important, for one of them will mate with a young queen bee. Bees mate in the air, and soon after a drone has mated with a queen bee, he dies. The queen bee returns to her hive and starts to lay eggs.

The worker bees are smaller than either the queen or drones but they do all the work of the large family. They are the female bees that serve the queen, clean the hive, and store up food for the winter. On their back legs they have pollen baskets in which pollen—the dust-like substance which comes from the center of certain flowers— is packed and carried. They also have stiff, wiry spines with which they remove the pollen from their baskets. On the front legs they have wax pinchers which they use in building the honeycomb.

121

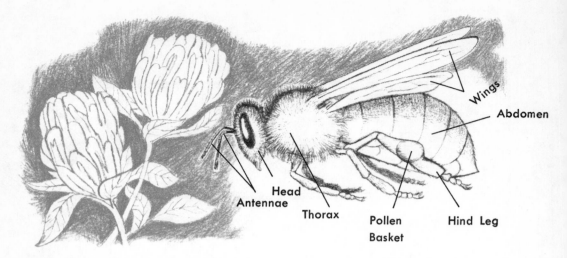

Wings

Abdomen

Head

Antennae

Thorax

Pollen
Basket

Hind Leg

The queen lays two kinds of eggs. The eggs which she lays in the drone cells hatch into drones. The rest of her eggs become either workers or queens. The workers and queens are the same kind of larvae at first; whether they grow to be queens or female workers depends on the way they are fed. All of the larvae are tiny white grubs which look nothing like grown honeybees.

For the first three days the worker bee grubs are fed bee jelly, a whitish substance which is spit up by the workers. For the next three days nectar and pollen from flowers are added, then their cells are covered over and closed up. The grubs wrap themselves in a heavy coating and go into their pupa stage, but in about fifteen days they come out of their closed cells as full grown worker bees.

Some of the grubs are fed bee jelly for six days instead of three, and they grow into queens instead of workers. It is easy to tell which cells have the baby queens in them because the workers have made these cells larger and they stick out like swollen bumps.

Before a new queen hatches, the old queen takes most of her old workers with her and leaves to find a new home. This keeps the number of bees in a hive from becoming too large. When a bee family goes out looking for a new home, it is said to be *swarming*. Many of the workers cling together, making a large cone-like formation about the queen. Other workers search carefully for a good place. which may be in a hollow tree, or perhaps a new hive which a beekeeper has set out. In fact beekeepers usually watch for the bees to swarm, then brush them into a new hive. As soon as the queen is captured, the other bees follow her. The workers start at once making brood cells in the new home, and the queen soon begins to lay eggs again.

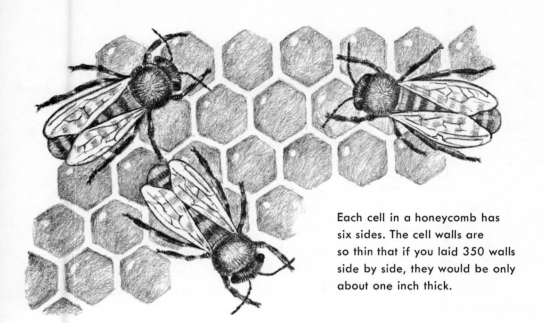

Each cell in a honeycomb has six sides. The cell walls are so thin that if you laid 350 walls side by side, they would be only about one inch thick.

As soon as a young queen hatches, she looks for other queen cells, tears them open, and kills the young queens inside. If two queens in a hive hatch at the same time, one is almost sure to sting the other to death. A new queen bee soon mates and begins to lay eggs. Sometimes she may lay more than a thousand eggs a day.

When the young worker bees first come out from their cells, they are very hungry and gorge on honey which the older bees have made from the nectar of flowers. After a few days, the young bees start to work. At first they are not strong enough to fly out and gather pollen and nectar. Their first task is to provide wax for the comb builders. Quietly they cling with their feet to the inside of the hive while the wax seeps out of the wax pockets on their abdomens and small balls of wax are pinched off and used by the comb builders.

Some young worker bees become comb builders, too. Others become bee nurses, housekeepers, food gatherers, or guards. Others help heat and ventilate the hive. In such a large family, many workers are needed and there are many jobs to do.

On cool days, some worker bees form a blanket over the brood cells to help keep the babies warm. A row of workers stationed near the slit-like door of the hive provide the ventilating system for the hive by fanning their wings rapidly. This forces fresh air through the hive. It is good exercise for the worker bees that will soon be

123

carrying nectar and pollen, for they must begin to gather food as soon as their wings are strong enough.

Other workers serve as guards for the hive and sniff at every bee that enters, for bees from other hives are not allowed inside. If a bumblebee should go into a honeybee hive, the guards would send it right out again.

When a worker leaves the hive to collect pollen and nectar from flowers, it may need to hunt a little to find the right flowers but when it flies back to the hive it goes the most direct way. This is the reason that people began to call the shortest and most direct way a *bee line*.

A bee family works on only one kind of flower at a time. For example, when a bee family is making clover honey, the bees of that hive visit only clover flowers. Later on, when making buckwheat honey they visit only buckwheat flowers. This is fortunate for the plants on which they work. In that way the pollen that the bees carry is not wasted but goes to other plants of the same kind where it is needed. Many plants will not produce seeds unless pollen from the same kind of plants is brought to them in some way. So bees are important to us in pollinizing plants, as well as in producing honey.

All summer the worker bees work hard in the fields to gather food for the hive. While they are packing their pollen baskets they also suck nectar from flowers. Juices in the mouths of the bees change the nectar to honey, which is carried in their crops. When the workers return to the hive they deposit the honey in the cells of the combs. By fall, they have a good supply of honey, enough to last them as food through the winter. It is from this winter food supply, which the bees make in such large quantities, that we get our honey.

During the winter only certain members of the bee family are allowed to live. All drones are stung to death, and any workers which are no longer useful are also cast from the hive. Only the queen and the strong workers are allowed to live through the winter.

When the weather first turns cold, the bees arrange themselves in the form of a hollow ball which makes it easier for them to keep warm. This ball of bees hangs from a layer of honeycomb so that their winter supply of food is close to them.

A Famous Jumper

A GRASSHOPPER can jump forty times its own length. Imagine jumping forty times your own length. If a man could jump as far for his size, he could cover a whole mile in about twenty jumps.

It is the grasshopper's long, strong, hind legs that enable it to jump so far. However, like other insects,

Notice the threadlike antennae of these long-horned grasshoppers. Grasshoppers can jump many times their own length.

a grasshopper has six legs, which it uses well in walking. Because of a sticky substance on its feet, it even can walk straight up a smooth wall.

Besides being a famous jumper, this insect, also, is a good flier and does most of its traveling by flying. Most grasshoppers have four wings, two of which are stiff and serve as wing covers for the other two. When not in use, a grasshopper's wings are folded back against its body.

If you have ever tried to catch a grasshopper, doubtless you have found that it is not easy. A grasshopper has so many eyes that it can see in every direction at once. On each side of its head there is a big compound eye, made up of many small six-sided eyes. There, also, is a small simple eye in front of each compound eye, and another in the middle of the insect's head. With so many eyes, it is no wonder that a grasshopper can see so well, even though it cannot turn its head from side to side as many other insects are able to do.

There are two well-known types of grasshoppers. One, called the long-horned or meadow grasshopper, has fine wavy feelers, or antennae, which are longer than its body. This kind belongs to the same family as the katydid but, instead of living in trees as the katydid

L. Chace

The short, stiff antennae, or
horns, of this magnified grasshopper
tell you it is a short-horned
grasshopper, or locust. A locust
is one of the most destructive
insects we have.

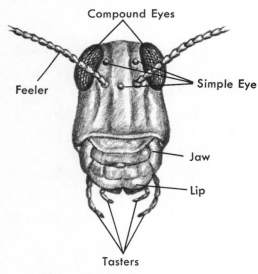

Compound Eyes

Feeler

Simple Eye

Jaw

Lip

Tasters

The upper lips of a grasshopper
are notched in the middle.
The jaws close together
from the sides. This enables
grasshoppers to cut and chew food.
They can give quite a hard pinch
with their jaws and often are
called biting insects.

does, it lives on the ground like other grasshoppers. The short-horned grasshopper, also common in our fields and meadows, is often called a *locust*. It has short, stiff antennae. In many ways, however, these two kinds of grasshoppers are much alike.

Grasshoppers like to eat grass. They cling to the blades of grass as they eat, holding them in an up-and-down position by little "fingers" at the sides of their mouths. The grass is cut by the sharp edges of their jaws.

Grasshoppers spit out a brown liquid that looks like tobacco juice. This liquid, which has an unpleasant odor, helps them to digest their food.

Although a grasshopper has no skeleton on the inside of its body, it has a smooth, shiny, firm coating on the outside which serves as a protection. It has a strange way of breathing. Air is taken in through tiny openings, smaller than pin holes, in its abdomen.

The short-horned grasshopper has its ears on its abdomen. They are round pieces of tissue, and are protected by the wings of the insect when the wings are at rest. The males make a grating noise by rubbing their hind legs against the edges of their stiff wings.

Like katydids, long-horned grasshoppers have ears on their front legs, just below the first joint. The males make a noise, or *sing*, by rubbing their wings together. The males of both the long-horned and short-horned grasshoppers attract the females with their songs. The females usually make no sound.

When a mother grasshopper is ready to lay her eggs, she makes a hole about an inch deep in the ground. There she lays masses of eggs which are held together by a sticky substance. The eggs usually are laid in the fall and hatch in the spring.

When the young grasshoppers, which are called *nymphs,* hatch, they are pale and delicate. At first they have no wings, but as the grasshoppers grow, the wings begin to develop and grow larger and larger. The insects also shed their coats for new, larger ones.

While the long-horned grasshoppers eat leaves and stems, they usually do not harm crops.

If you see a huge swarm of grasshoppers flying low over a field of grain, they are probably short-horned grasshoppers or locusts. Some kinds of locusts, such as Rocky Mountain locusts, can destroy a whole field of grain.

The top picture shows a field of corn before locusts came swarming over it. The bottom picture shows the field after the locusts had gone. Do you see how locusts can destroy a whole field of grain?

127

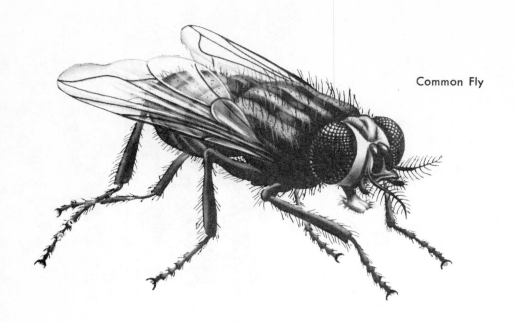

Common Fly

Two Insect Enemies

THE HOUSEFLY is a very rude insect, slipping into our homes uninvited. Then it stands with all six of its dirty feet on our food and sucks the nice, juicy part. Worse than that, it leaves germs wherever it goes.

The mosquito also is a rude insect enemy, biting people without so much as a warning. You may be sure that if a mosquito bites you, it is a female. Male mosquitoes live on plant juices. We do not see the males often because they do not bite or suck blood for food. In fact, they have no sharp mouth parts with which they could pierce a hole in the skin. Female mosquitoes, however, suck blood whenever they can. Their sucking tubes have sharp points like needles with which they puncture the skin of a victim.

Flies and mosquitoes are very unpopular. They have become known as enemies of people because they carry and spread disease germs. These insects grow from eggs into adult insects in such a short time that many generations of them live in a single season.

Flies and mosquitoes have only two wings, but, like other insects, they have six legs and three body parts—head, thorax, and abdomen. The legs and wings are fastened to the thorax.

Of course, some kinds of flies are really helpful to people because they carry pollen from flower to flower much like bees do. There are other flies that eat many harmful insects. Of the many thousands of

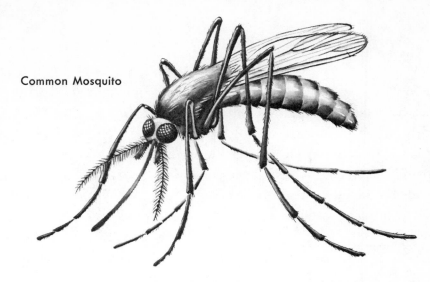

Common Mosquito

different kinds of flies in the United States, only a small number are really our enemies.

One of the best known and harmful flies is the common housefly. It lives all over the world, wherever people live, for the garbage that people leave helps these flies to breed.

Although the fly has no nose, its antennae act as smellers and a fly can detect odors that are a long distance away. Instead of a mouth, a fly has a small trunk, or *proboscis,* with which it sucks up its food.

A mother housefly lays many eggs in manure piles or garbage dumps. She selects these filthy places because the fly larvae depend on manure or garbage for their food during the first week of their lives. The larvae hatch within a few hours after the eggs are laid. They grow fast and in about six days they get brown coats, which make them look like grains of wheat. This is their pupa stage which lasts for about five days. The adult flies develop from the pupae and never grow any bigger than they are at first. The mother flies soon are ready to lay eggs.

Since mother flies lay so many eggs and it takes less than two weeks for a fly to grow up, it is easy to understand why there are so many flies in the world.

If you have tried to slip up to a fly with a swatter, you know how quickly it can dart away before you have a chance to hit it. The fly's head is almost all eyes, and it is able to see in every direction at once. On each side of its head is a large compound eye made of thousands of small eyes. A fly's eyes are its best means of protection.

People try to get rid of flies by cleaning up garbage and manure piles, by screening windows and doors to keep them from their homes, and by using chemicals.

One kind of mosquito carries the virus of yellow fever and another carries the parasite which causes malaria. Mosquitoes seem to prefer to suck the blood from a broad, smooth expanse of flesh, like the human back. They also prefer to bite warm, slightly moist flesh. If a female gets in air that has blown past a human being, she can smell food immediately with her antennae.

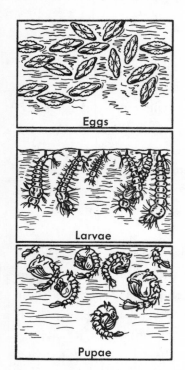

Eggs

Larvae

Pupae

Mosquitoes, like flies, go through four stages while growing up and their life-cycle may also be very short. They grow quickly from eggs to adults. A typical life history is that of the Culex, or common mosquito.

A pool of water that yesterday was so still it looked like a mirror, today may be alive with mosquito larvae. We wonder where these tiny "wrigglers" came from. When we learn what they are, we know that a day or two ago a mother mosquito laid her eggs on the surface of the water. The eggs stuck together and floated on the water like a flat little raft until they hatched.

Adult

For a few days the wrigglers hang in the water eating little particles. Then they turn into pupae often called "tumblers." In about five more days they emerge on the top of the water as mosquitoes.

A mosquito that stands on its head when it bites and has spotted wings is the kind that can carry malaria. It is known as the Anopheles mosquito. It is found more commonly in the southern part of the United States and in tropical regions. Most mosquitoes that live in the northern part of the United States do not transmit disease.

Culex Mosquito   Anopheles Mosquito   Aedes Mosquito

The Anopheles mosquito does not have the malaria parasite until it bites a person who has malaria. After sucking it in with the sick person's blood, this mosquito carries the parasite in its stomach. There it lives and develops for a week or two, before moving forward into the saliva. It then may be passed on to people whom the mosquito bites.

The Aedes is the name of the mosquito that carries yellow fever as the Anopheles carries malaria. During the Spanish American War the United States sent troops to Cuba. There many of our soldiers became sick with yellow fever. Army doctors were sent to Cuba to find out what caused the disease. By experimenting they proved that the bite of the Aedes mosquito caused it.

At the time the Panama Canal was built these mosquitoes were a terrible pest, causing many deaths among the workers. Not until the Americans learned how to destroy them was it possible for people to live at the canal. Without workers the canal could not have been completed.

Now people have learned several ways of killing numbers of mosquitoes. Sometimes they pour oil on top of standing water where these insects lay their eggs. The wrigglers and tumblers come in contact with the oil when they came to the surface to breathe and are poisoned. We do not pour oil on large bodies of water, such as rivers and lakes, because it would be harmful to the many kinds of animals living there. Fish and many water insects eat the mosquito wrigglers. Lakes and rivers that are full of fish usually do not have many young mosquitoes in them. Bats, birds, and dragon flies are also enemies of grown mosquitoes.

People have spent a great deal of money trying to get rid of the two insect enemies, flies and mosquitoes. Various powerful chemicals are used to kill them. It is not wise, however, to use powerful chemicals without careful thought because they can also kill many helpful insects and can be harmful to humans. In spite of the effort of people to get rid of these insect enemies, there still are many of them.

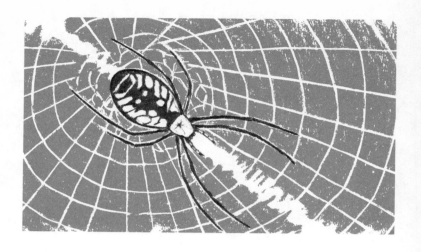

ANIMALS WITH EIGHT LEGS

Mother Eight-legs Spins a Web

CAN you imagine a nest with five hundred eggs in it? The next time you are in a flower garden, look carefully at each dead plant you find. Fastened to one of them may be a sac-like and well-lined waterproof nest a mother garden spider has made. In it may be hundreds of tiny, pearly white spider eggs.

Soon after a mother spider makes her sac-like nest and lays her eggs, she dies. The baby spiders hatch inside the nest. When they first hatch, it is too cold for them to leave the nest and they are hungry. There is no one to bring them food so the older, stronger baby spiders eat the younger, weaker ones. Since only the strong spiders survive, there is plenty of room in the nest for them.

The baby spiders grow so fast that soon they are too big for their outside body coverings. The coverings are hard and will not stretch so the spiders split their old suits and crawl out of them. Under the old suits are new ones.

In the spring the spiders leave their nest and go off in different directions. A female spider may climb to the top of a little shrub. She is hungry and knows she must have food. Instinct tells her what to do next.

The spider spins a thread of silk and fastens it to a branch. As she spins the thread out longer and longer, she lets herself down by it. With the help of a breeze, soon she is able to swing herself across to a nearby plant. There she fastens the other end of the thread. Now she has a bridge to walk on and the beginning of a web.

The spider spins other threads that cross the first and fastens the ends to other branches. Finally she has a framework that looks like the rim and spokes of a wheel. The threads are stretched tight and fastened where they cross. Then the

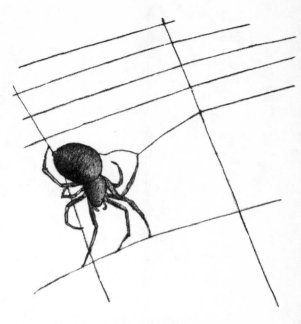

With her hind legs, the spider draws silk from the glands in her abdomen and places it on the web.

spider begins at the center and spins a thread around and around, going farther and farther out until, after five or six complete turns, she arrives at the rim. Where this thread crosses the spokes, it, too, is fastened securely. This gives her a frame to walk on while she spins another kind of thread into her web.

All the threads the spider has put into the web so far have been dry, but now she begins from the outside and spins a new round-and-round thread in toward the center. This new thread is sticky and quite closely woven. The old threads are cut away as the new sticky threads are put in. At last, after the spider has spun more threads across the front and back of the web, it is finished. It takes a garden spider about an hour to spin her web. This kind of web is called an orb-web.

Now the spider moves to the center of the web and waits. Soon a fly flies into the web. It struggles but the sticky threads hold it fast. Quickly the spider bites the fly with her two poison fangs and paralyzes it. She sucks out the liquid part of the fly's body. Then she cuts away part of the web to let the rest of the body fall. Carefully she mends the web and waits for another insect to be caught.

The Jumping Spider climbs to the top of a plant. Her silk spinners float upward and a breeze carries her through the air.

As a garden spider spins more webs and eats more insects, she grows larger and larger. She may outgrow her hard outer covering several times before she becomes an adult spider. Then she will be almost an inch long and will be black with spots of bright orange. The front part of her body will be covered with silvery white hairs.

A garden spider has eight eyes. Instead of jaws, she has fangs with which to poison insects. She breathes through two lung slits in the lower part of her abdomen.

The male garden spider is much smaller and has less coloring. He does not live long for after a female and male spider mate, the female usually eats him. Male spiders, like drones of the bee family, do no work.

In the fall, the female garden spider lays eggs in a sac. During the winter, food is scarce and the spider dies before her eggs hatch.

There are thousands of kinds of spiders. All spiders have eight legs and two body parts. But spiders vary in other ways. Most spiders spin webs but some, such as the trap door spider, do not.

Spiders spin different kinds of webs. The grass spider makes a funnel web. The house spider weaves a cobweb.

The Trap Door Spider does not spin a web. She digs a little tube in the ground and weaves a round door over it. When she is hungry, she hides under the door until she feels the quiver of an insect passing. Then she pops open the door and pulls the insect inside.

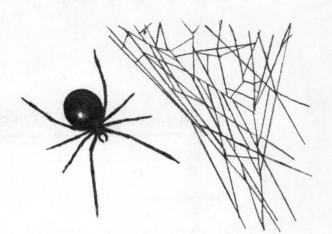

The Black Widow Spider is about a half-inch long. Her shiny, black body has a red mark, shaped like an hour glass, on the under side of the abdomen.

Some spiders do not fasten their egg sac to a dead plant. They fasten the egg sac to their own bodies and carry it around with them. When the baby spiders hatch, they climb on the mother's back and cling to her until they are ready to go off by themselves to find food.

Spiders have several enemies, but the wasp is perhaps the worst one. A mother wasp does not use the spider for food for herself but stores it in her burrow or cells for the baby wasps. First the wasp stings the spider until it is helpless; then it lays eggs on the spider's body. As soon as the eggs hatch, the baby wasps have spider food. Some wasps use the trap door spider's home for a nursery. Many birds also eat spiders.

Although spiders poison the insects which they eat, their bites are usually harmless to us. Of the spiders found in the United States, the black widow and the brown house spider have poisons that are harmful to people. Most people kill every spider they see yet spiders help us by destroying insects that may harm our crops.

Spiders also help us in another way. The silk they weave is used in making the delicate cross-lines of telescopes and in other instruments where a strong but very fine thread is needed.

Some kinds of spiders, like the tarantula, hunt for food instead of trapping it in a web or under a trap door. The tarantula is hairy and may grow to be several inches long. It chases and catches insects, lizards, and sometimes even baby birds for food.

135

ANIMALS WITH NO LEGS

The Animal that Eats Dirt

DURING a hard rain, earthworms are sometimes seen lying on top of the ground. They often come out during a heavy rain to keep from being drowned. Birds and some other animals, especially moles, eat many of these worms.

Earthworms often are called angleworms, and sometimes "night crawlers." The large ones frequently found on top of the ground at night make good bait for fishermen. These sometimes are ten inches long.

Earthworms move about a great deal in their search for food. If the soil is soft, they may push their way through it, but if the soil is hard, they *eat* their way through it. Their bodies digest some of the substances in the soil, and they leave the rest on top of the ground near their holes. They, also, eat bits of leaves or other vegetable material that they find on the surface of the ground.

Usually you have to dig in the ground to find earthworms because they do not come out often except at night. Even then they leave their tails sticking in their holes and by this means find their way back. Earthworms have no eyes, no ears, and no sense of smell so they have to find their way about entirely by feel and taste.

The earthworm's body is made up of little parts or segments fitting

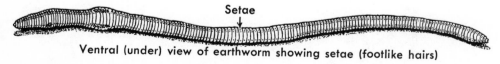

Setae

Ventral (under) view of earthworm showing setae (footlike hairs)

end to end against one another. Some earthworms have as many as 150 or more segments. On each segment are four pairs of hairlike bristles which are so small that they can hardly be seen, but they help the worm in crawling. An earthworm can grow a new head or tail if

136

either of these parts happens to be cut off. But it cannot live if more than about fifteen of its head segments are removed.

Earthworms are soft and easily crushed because they have no hard parts to protect them. They both drink and breathe through their skins; if their bodies are not kept moist they soon die. When the topsoil is moist, they stay near the surface but when the soil is dry, they go down deeper and deeper until they find damp earth. In the winter they go down below the frost line to keep from freezing. During very cold or dry weather earthworms sometimes go down as deep as eight feet. There a number of them may roll up together in a ball.

On a band about a third of the way back on the earthworm's body a cocoon is formed which protects its eggs. This cover moves forward slowly much as a ring is taken off a person's finger, and on its way forward, it receives the eggs lying on the skin of the worm, and forms a little sac with the eggs in it. This sac keeps the eggs moist until they hatch and then protects the small worms until they are big enough to leave the sac.

Although earthworms do not have eyes or ears, their sensitive bodies can tell daylight from dark. They can also feel vibrations with their bodies, and will crawl back into their holes if the ground around them is jarred. They have crops and gizzards much like those of chickens only much smaller. The crop stores dirt as it is swallowed and lets it into the gizzard, a little at a time, where it is ground up. The greater part of the dirt, which cannot be used as food, is discarded.

Earthworms are of great service to plants because by grinding up dirt it is made into better soil. Also, they bring to the surface particles of soil from lower levels. This is much like the work the farmer tries to do with his tools. The earthworm does it more slowly, but better, and often goes down to much greater depths than the farmer can reach with his plow.

Through its tunnels, the earthworm helps air and water get into the earth. In hard ground, the roots of plants may even follow the worm holes. Earthworms, also, carry bits of vegetable material into the ground, which helps to enrich the soil. These queer little worms truly deserve a place high on the list of our most useful animals.

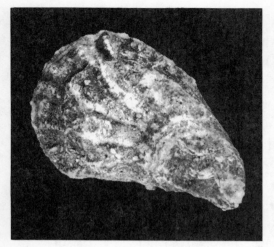
L. Chace

ANIMALS WITH TWO SHELLS

An Animal Without a Head

THE oyster is an animal which has a mouth, lips, heart, and gills, but no head, hands, or feet. It looks much like a lump of soft flesh between a hinged pair of shells.

The shells are hinged together at the back and open and close like the covers of a book. The open and closing mechanism consists of two parts. One is made up of strong muscles within the soft parts of the animal and the other is a tough ribbonlike band which unites the two parts of the shell. The muscles pull the shells together and the band pulls them apart.

Oysters can get along without feet, because they spend most of their lives fastened to something solid at the bottom of the ocean. They live along the ocean shores in bays or at the mouths of rivers. The depth of the water in which they live may be very shallow or as deep as ninety feet. They cannot move about even to search for food. But the ocean water supplies them with both food and oxygen.

Oysters' gills not only enable them to get air from the water, but they, also, serve as food carriers and, for some oysters, as baby carriages as well. The gills are folds of the body which extend into a cavity through which water can flow freely. Little hairlike bodies on the inside of the tube fan the water to the gills. After oxygen is taken in by the gills and carbon dioxide is given off, the water is then fanned out of the oyster's body through another tube.

The gills have a sticky covering which gathers tiny animals and plants from the water as the water currents flow by. These little victims are food for the oyster. About a gallon of water goes through the gills of an oyster in an hour.

138

Most European oysters hatch their eggs in their gills and carry their young there for the first few days. American oysters give off their eggs directly into the sea where they hatch by themselves. Baby oysters are so tiny that they look like specks in the water. They swim about for a day or two then settle down to something solid. There they attach themselves and spend the rest of their lives. Many of them are eaten by other animals, but a mother oyster lives several years, and each year lays several million eggs so there are many baby oysters left to grow up.

Raising oysters has become an important industry. There are many beds where the oysters are carefully protected. But there are not as many oysters now as there once were because they are being used faster than they are being produced.

Oysters have other enemies besides man. Starfish are one of their worst enemies, and men who have oyster beds try to keep starfish out. The oyster drill, a little snail that bores into their shells and sucks out their soft bodies, is another enemy of oysters.

Boys and girls who live along the East Coast, especially those near Chesapeake Bay, may have seen oysters being gathered from the ocean. Perhaps they, also, have seen oyster farmers scattering shells in the water on which the baby oysters may attach themselves when they settle to the bottom.

A kind of shellfish related to the oyster, and generally called a pearl oyster, can make gem pearls which real oysters cannot do. While pearls sometimes are found in edible oysters, they are of poor quality.

The way in which pearls are formed is very interesting. Sometimes the water carries a grain of sand or some other bit of hard material between the hinged shells of the oyster. There it lodges because this little animal has no way of removing the sand. Instead it gradually covers the grain with a heavy coating which is like the inside of its shell. Soon a second coat is formed on top of the first one. By and by the grain of sand has many coats of the shiny shell-like covering over it. In time it is these coverings that make a beautiful pearl inside the oyster. Several kinds of shellfish form pearls in this same manner.

Because oysters, pearl-oysters, clams, and mussels all have two shells, they belong to a group of animals called bivalves.

139

Land Snail

L. Chace

ANIMALS WITH ONE SHELL

An Animal that Carries Its House on Its Back

THERE are big, little, and medium-sized snails. They may live in the ocean, in ponds, or in gardens. No matter where they live or how big they are, they always move slowly. A snail has to carry its house, or shell, with it wherever it goes. It has only one foot. But there is little danger that a snail will fall along the way, for its foot is a big part of its body. Other animals may travel faster, but few are more sure of arriving.

There are many kinds of snails. Some snails eat other animals while other snails eat only plants. Some snails that live in the water breathe with gills, but others have lungs.

The tadpole snail, which is shaped like a tadpole, is one of those which live in fresh water ponds. It has lungs so it must go to the surface to breathe, although it finds its food in the bottom of the water. This snail builds its own small ladder in the water. The ladder is made of threads of slimy material and reaches from the bottom to the surface of the pond. The tadpole snail climbs the ladder easily, then drops down again without using it.

This kind of snail lays many eggs in a jellylike mass. When the snails are hatched, their shells are very delicate. The babies eat much and grow fast. Soon their shells become hard and are then good protection for their soft bodies. Just as we must eat certain foods to have good teeth, snails must eat certain foods to have good shells.

The periwinkle is a snail which lives in salt water. Its shell, which is about the size of a man's thumb nail, is a yellowish brown color. It is often found on rocks and seaweed along the shore of the Atlantic Ocean.

The queen conch is much larger than the periwinkle. It may be more than a foot long and weigh several pounds. The body of this snail is used for food in some countries. Meat is used as bait, since this is one of the snails that eats meat.

A land snail lays a sidewalk as it travels. From the entire under surface of its foot a slimy substance is given off as it moves from place to place, and it leaves a thin layer of this slimy material behind it as it moves along.

If the weather becomes very dry, a garden snail pulls its foot inside its shell and seals up the opening with a layer of this slimy material. In this way the snail is protected from drying up. In the winter, land snails dig down into the ground, seal themselves in their shells, and go to sleep until spring.

Besides their shells, land snails have two pairs of tentacles, or feelers, to help them in protecting themselves. One pair, which is longer than the other, has an eye at the end of each feeler.

One kind of land snail is called the edible snail because it is so often used for food. In France and Spain these snails, which are about the size of large strawberries, are raised on snail farms. The snails are fed on vegetables which they have no trouble in eating because of the hundreds of sharp teeth on their tongues.

Like other snails, the Mediterranean Snail uses its shell as its house. But what we call a snail's house, or shell, is really its skeleton.

Chicago Natural History Museum

141

L. Chace

ANIMALS WITH SPINY SKINS

Neither Stars nor Fishes

STARFISH does not seem a very good name for a group of animals that are neither stars nor fishes. Still these strange animals usually have five arms like a star and they do live in the ocean.

They belong to the many kinds of small animals with sharp spines called spiny-skinned animals. The starfish's spiny skin is its best protection from its enemies.

Like other animals of its kind, the starfish has a system of many water-filled tubes in its body. Tube feet, also, extend out from the water tubes on the under side of the starfish's arms. The starfish uses its tube feet to move about and to catch its food.

Suction cups on the ends of these feet make it possible for the starfish to walk over slippery rocks. Although starfish have gills with which to breathe, the walls of their tube feet could be called their lungs because oxygen and carbon dioxide also pass in and out through them.

Grown men may find it hard to open an oyster or clam shell, but the little starfish has a special way of doing it. It humps its body over the oyster and attaches some of its tube feet to each of its victim's two shells. Then it presses its tube feet down tight and they grasp the shells with the suction cups.

When its tube feet are well fastened, the starfish begins a steady pull on both shells. If the feet which are doing the pulling become tired, other tube feet continue the pull. They may pull for a long time. But at last the muscles of the oyster become so tired that they weaken, and the two shells spread open. The starfish then places its mouth, which is in the center of the lower side of its body and

142

which leads directly to the stomach, over the body of its victim. It turns its stomach partly inside out in order to surround the soft parts of the oyster and slowly digests its meal.

As oysters are one of the most common foods of the starfish, the people who gather oysters for food are not pleased to find starfish in their oyster beds. These men have tried many ways of protecting oysters from their starfish enemies. Sometimes nets are placed around the oyster beds to keep out the starfish.

A starfish can turn itself over by its tube feet much as you turn handsprings. Since it has no regular head or tail, it can move in any direction and still not be going backwards. Starfish do most of their moving about in the night. During the daytime they rest hidden among the rocks. Sometimes they burrow in the sand until their bodies are almost covered.

Because starfish babies do not have arms, they look quite different from their parents. When they are first hatched, they swim around near the surface of the ocean for a few days before they settle down to the bottom to grow up.

A mother starfish may lay thousands of eggs although many of them never have a chance to hatch, because they become food for other animals. If a starfish loses a part of its body, it grows a new part to take the place of the one it has lost. Because of this, a starfish can be badly injured and still recover.

Starfish are often brightly colored. Not all of them have five points or arms. Sea urchins and sea cucumbers are relatives of the starfish which like all the other spiny-skinned animals are able to grow new body parts if some of them are lost in an accident.

American Museum of Natural History

The Sea Urchin and the Sea Cucumber are relatives of the Starfish.

Redbeard Sponge

SPONGES

A Skeleton in Your House

MANY PEOPLE use sponges in their homes—in the bathroom, kitchen, or perhaps in the garage. Sponges are soft and soak up a great deal of water which is released as they are squeezed. Often they are used for washing windows, woodwork, or automobiles. But many people do not know that a sponge is the skeleton of an animal.

The first story in this book explains that it is hard to tell whether some living things are plants or animals. For many years people believed that sponges were plants because they looked like plants and they seemed to be growing from the bottom of the ocean. Then, for a time, sponges were believed to be a curious combination of plant and animal life and they were called plant-animals. Later, after learning how sponges breathe and get their food, scientists determined that they were really animals.

The sponge gets its shape from its skeleton, the small openings of which are filled with a jellylike substance when the sponge is living. The skeleton holds the jellylike mass together and keeps it from collapsing. This mass contained in the sponge's skeleton is very active. It swallows many gallons of water a day taking the air and tiny animals from it. Then it spouts the water out again like a fountain. The larger tubes, or canals, are lined with very tiny hairlike paddles that push the water through the sponge, much as water is pushed through the tubes of an oyster.

There are many kinds of sponges, some small and soft, and others hard and as big as a barrel. They grow in many shapes and colors. Although most of them grow in the salt water of the ocean, a few kinds

144

live in fresh water or streams. One interesting kind is called the finger sponge because each branch is about six inches long and shaped like a finger. The most beautiful sponge is Venus's-flower-basket which grows about a foot high and is shaped like a tube. The skeleton of this strange sponge looks like silver-colored glass.

The only sponge of great importance, however, is the ordinary bath sponge which is so useful around a home. These have been found in greatest numbers in the Mediterranean Sea, and off the coasts of Florida and the Bahama Islands. Tarpon Springs, on the west coast of Florida, is a leading center of the sponge industry.

Sponges usually are gathered off the bottom of the oceans by deep sea divers. But some times they are snagged in shallow water by special long-handled hooks which the sponge fishermen carry in their boats. Live bath sponges look much like raw beef liver when they are first taken out of the water. They are hung in the sun until the jelly-like mass inside the skeleton begins to dry. Then they are pounded and washed, and dried again.

Although this strange animal produces eggs which hatch into baby sponges, the mother sponge also may grow bumps or *buds* on her body which break off to form new sponges. If a sponge is cut into several pieces, each piece usually will grow into a new sponge. After baby sponges are hatched from eggs they swim about for a time before they attach themselves to something solid on the bottom of the ocean.

Most animals will not eat sponges because of their unpleasant taste and odor. The sponge crab wears a sponge on its back. With this covering other animals are not liable to attack it, and it can find its food easily without being noticed.

Sponges have become more and more scarce in recent years in spite of the fact that other animals do not like to eat them and that they reproduce young sponges in two different ways. There is a disease which sometimes attacks sponges often causing them to die. Also, too many sponges may be gathered in one place so that there are few left to grow up.

Substitutes are now being made which have taken over many of the uses for which we once depended on sponges. These substitutes follow largely the plan of the sponge skeleton.

The Parade of Plants

As we have been reading about the Parade of Living Things, we have learned much about animals. Now we are going to read about another part of that parade—the Parade of Plants.

You know that all living things are either plants or animals. You know, too, that plants and animals are alike in some ways. They grow. They need food, air, water, and some warmth. They can produce others like themselves.

You also know how plants and animals are different. Most animals can move. They get their food by eating other animals and plants. Most plants cannot move. Green plants make their own food from substances in soil and water and from gases in the air.

But not all plants are green. Not all plants can make their own food. There are many kinds of plants and they differ in many ways.

Some plants are so tiny they can be seen only under a microscope. Bacteria and yeasts are plants like these.

The oldest and largest living things in the world are also plants. Kelp, a seaweed that grows in the ocean, often reaches a length of more than 100 feet. The giant sequoia trees of California tower to the sky. One of them, called the General Sherman tree, is nearly 300 feet tall and is more than thirty feet thick at its base. It is believed to be more than 3,000 years old.

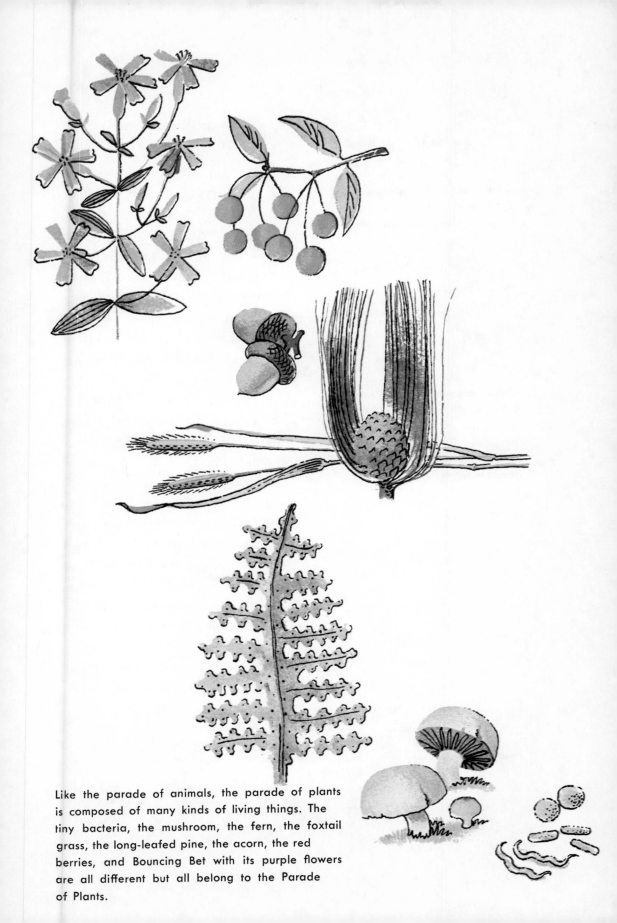

Like the parade of animals, the parade of plants is composed of many kinds of living things. The tiny bacteria, the mushroom, the fern, the foxtail grass, the long-leafed pine, the acorn, the red berries, and Bouncing Bet with its purple flowers are all different but all belong to the Parade of Plants.

Many Plants Are Green

Daisy   Tomato

Green plants make their own food from water, air, and minerals in the presence of light.

Some Are Not Green

Mushroom   Yeast (enlarged)

Non-green plants depend upon things which are alive or have been alive for their food. Mushrooms use decaying plant and animal matter in soil. Yeast plants feed on sugar.

Green Plants and Non-Green Plants

LIKE animals, plants are divided into two main groups—plants that have seeds and plants that do not have seeds. Each main group is divided into smaller groups.

One of the most important divisions is between green plants and plants that are not green.

Green plants are *independent*. They make their own food from air, water, minerals, and light.

Non-green plants are *dependent*. They cannot make their own food but depend on other things for the food they need.

All forms of animal life depend upon green plants for food. You drink milk. You eat eggs and meat. The cattle that provide the milk and meat eat grain and grass. Eggs come from chickens that eat grain. Everything we eat, except salt and water, can be traced back to green plants.

Non-green plants, like yeast and mushrooms, also depend upon green plants for food.

The seeds of most kinds of seed plants develop from flowers.

Other kinds of seed plants have cones instead of flowers.

Some kinds of plants have no flowers, seeds, or cones.

Aster   Pine Tree   Fern

How Some Plants Reproduce Themselves Without Seeds

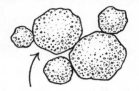
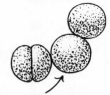

| Mushroom | Fern | A Yeast Plant (enlarged) | A Bacterium (enlarged) |

Mushrooms and ferns develop tiny spores which produce new plants.

Yeast plants produce little buds which break off and grow into new plants.

Bacteria divide in halves, each half becoming a new separate plant.

Plants with Seeds and Seedless Plants

NO one ever picked a bouquet of fern flowers. Neither did anyone ever gather mushroom seeds. Ferns and mushrooms have neither flowers nor seeds. There are other plants too, that do not have flowers and seeds. The moss found on the moist, shady side of rocks is one of them. Most water plants are seedless. This seedless group includes the very tiny plants that can be seen only with a microscope and the very large ones such as kelp.

Perhaps you wonder how such plants produce new ones since they have no seeds. There are several ways. Very small plants may divide in halves, each half becoming a separate plant, in the same manner that the tiny animal, the amoeba, reproduces itself.

Yeast plants form little buds or bumps on their bodies. When the buds are big enough, they break off and become new yeast plants. Many of the seedless plants form tiny spores which, although different from seeds, develop into new plants if they reach the right places and have the right conditions for growth.

A seed plant is usually a flowering plant, and a flowering plant usually produces seeds. There are a few seed plants which produce cones. Your Christmas tree is an example. The sequoia is another. But there are not nearly as many kinds of cone-bearing plants as there are flowering plants.

Some flowering plants are small and others very large. One of the smallest is the duckweed plant that grows in lakes and ponds. The largest flowering plants are trees. Some tree flowers, like those of the cottonwood tree, are hard to find. Other tree flowers like those of the locust, horse chestnut, magnolia, and flowering fruit trees are colorful and beautiful.

149

Plant Families

SCIENTISTS have divided plants into families. Plants which have flowers much alike are in the same family. You would expect members of the same family to look alike in other ways, too, and some of them do have stems or leaves much alike. For example, the members of the mint family have square stems and the grass family has long slender leaves.

The rose family is an interesting one. It has very big members and very small members. The strawberry plant is one of the smallest members and the apple tree is one of the largest. Did you know that the apple and the strawberry are relatives of the roses in your garden? In fact, they all belong to the same plant family. They all have flowers which are very much alike.

Members of the Rose Family

APRICOTS   STRAWBERRIES   CHERRIES

PEARS

BLACKBERRIES

LETTUCE

ASTERS

DAHLIAS

DANDELIONS

ARTICHOKE

Members of the Composite Family

Another of the plant families often is called the sunflower family although it has a much better name—the composite family. "Composite" means many together. All the kinds of plants in this family have many flowers arranged together in clusters or bouquets. The daisy, the dandelion, and the aster are members of this group.

You know that the parade of animal life has been going on for millions of years. The plant parade started millions of years ago, too. In fact, since animals depend upon plants for food, the plant parade must have started first.

By a careful study of the traces of plants left in the layers of rock in the earth's crust, scientists have been able to piece much of the story together. As is true of animals, the first plants were very small and simple and lived in water. They belonged to the seedless group. But these plants must have been able to make their own food, as there was no other food for them.

These plants lived in the age of the trilobite.

These plants lived when eryops was alive.

These plants lived when the dinosaur *stegosaurus* roamed earth.

These plants lived in the age of Neanderthal Man.

The first very simple plants were followed by larger green seedless ones. Some of them probably did not live in water, but all of them needed much moisture. Liverworts and mosses which we find growing on rocks today are relatives of those plants of long ago.

Then came still larger plants—horsetails, club mosses, and ferns. We have such plants now but they are much smaller than they once were. Long ago some of them were as large as our trees. Those plants were growing their best and biggest during the Age of Amphibians and the Age of Reptiles. In fact, the Age of Amphibians often is called the Coal Age because it was from the many huge plants of that time that our coal was formed.

The first seed plants were the cone-bearing ones, which came about the beginning of the Age of Reptiles. The flowering plants came along with the mammals. They grew very well and now, during the Age of Man, many of the families of flowering plants are better known and more appreciated than any other kinds of plants.

Like the parade of animals, our plant parade starts with the more highly developed and better known plants, and ends with some of the simple forms that many people do not know are plants. This, too, is an interesting parade. First come the plants with flowers. Then the ones with cones. Next come the plants that have no seeds, first the green ones without seeds, then the non-green ones without seeds.

PLANTS WITH SEEDS

Flowers and Their Helpers

WHY do plants have flowers? Is it to please our sense of smell? No, that is not the reason for many flowers have no fragrance and a few even have an unpleasant odor. Is it because their beauty pleases us? No, for many flowers are not beautiful. Plants have flowers to produce the seeds from which new plants will grow.

Let us examine the picture, on the next page, of an apple blossom. First notice the swollen bud that is ready to burst open. It is protected by a covering of tightly overlapping *sepals* which look something like tiny leaves. When the bud opens the sepals separate and the *petals* unfold. As with most flowers, the petals are the most beautifully colored parts. Toward the center of the flower note some threadlike stalks with little knobs on their tips. These stalks are called the *stamens*, and it is within the knobs, or sacs, that the *pollen* grains develop.

If you were to touch one of the knobs of a real apple blossom, you would find that the pollen is a fine yellow dust or powder that sticks to your finger. Although pollen usually is yellow, on some flowers such as tulips and poppies it is almost black. The pollen is necessary in developing seeds. We will say more about that after we have examined another part of the flower, which is in the very center, surrounded by the stamens. This is called the *pistil*. If you touch the upper broadened part of the pistil, called the *stigma*, you will find that it feels sticky. This is so it can better capture and hold the pollen that is needed. The lower part of the *pistil*, called the *ovary*, has a bulb-like shape, and is buried deep at the base of the flower, close to its stem. Within the ovary are several tiny, green balls called *ovules*. The ovules are the parts that grow into seeds, but first they must be fertilized by the contents from the pollen grains.

In some flowers, such as the violet, the pistil can use the pollen

153

This bee is gathering nectar.

which comes from the stamens of the same flower. The parts of these flowers are usually arranged so that their own pollen falls down upon their pistils. Thus they are self-pollinated. Many flowers, however, are fertilized by pollen from other flowers of their kind. Such flowers are cross-pollinated. Cross-pollination is important because it often produces stronger and better plants.

For cross-pollination many flowers have "helpers" to bring the pollen from other flowers. Bees and many kinds of flies are among the chief helpers. But humming birds, and some moths and butterflies also carry pollen to certain flowers. Almost every kind of flower has such helpers, and is able in some way to attract them.

In the apple blossom picture we see a bee that is about to settle down on the flower. She seems to

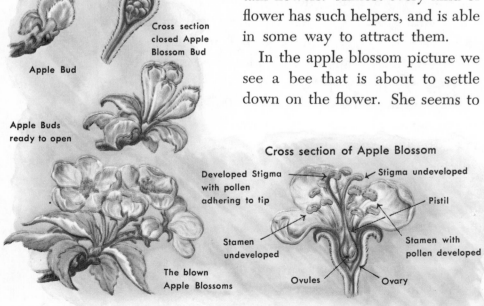

Apple Bud

Cross section closed Apple Blossom Bud

Apple Buds ready to open

Cross section of Apple Blossom

Developed Stigma with pollen adhering to tip

Stigma undeveloped

Pistil

Stamen undeveloped

Stamen with pollen developed

The blown Apple Blossoms

Ovules

Ovary

Stages in the Development of the Apple Blossom

be after something. Notice that she has some pollen on her back legs. She will help pollinate the flower. The bee does not know that she is helping the flower. Then why does she come to it?

The reason is that the bee is searching for food. Bees gather pollen, take it back to the hive and use it as food. Bees also gather a sweet liquid called *nectar*, which is stored deep down in the flower. It is from this liquid that the bee makes honey.

The fine odor of the flowers, and their beautiful colors also, are there for a purpose. And that purpose is to attract the bees or other insects which will help cross-pollinate them.

Since bees and butterflies work during the daytime, the flowers which depend upon them for help are more fragrant during the day than they are at night. And since moths do their work at night, the flowers which depend upon them for help are usually white and strongly scented, thus making it easier for the moths to find them.

Some flowers, like the skunk cabbage, have an unpleasant odor that probably is no more attractive to a bee or butterfly than it is to people. But even such flowers have their helpers. They are pollinated by flies.

Bee with pollen on legs

Honeybee with white clover

Bumblebee on red clover

Hawk moth on flower

Yucca moth and yucca plant

155

Bees and other pollinating insects seem always to work on only one kind of plant at a time. This is fortunate for the plants since the pollen that is carried would be of no use to a flower unless it came from a flower of its own kind. Let us see now how some kinds of flowers are pollinated by bees.

The bee comes to the flower with pollen on her body which she got while visiting another flower. As she brushes past the stigma, which she must do in order to reach the nectar, some of the pollen is caught by the stigma. Then she passes by the stamens which dust her body with a fresh supply of pollen. When she leaves to go for more nectar, she is ready to pollinate another flower.

Here is a very interesting story of a plant that failed to produce seed without its special little helpers. At one time the red clover did not grow in Australia. Seeds were brought from the United States and planted. The plants grew very well and produced fine flowers on them, but the flowers did not produce seeds. Again the following year clover seeds from the United States were planted, and again there were splendid flowers, but no seeds. Then someone discovered that the bumblebee is the special little helper that pollinates the flowers of the red clover. There were no bumblebees in Australia. The bumblebee is the only insect with a tongue long enough to reach the nectar of this flower. Other insects will not waste their time on this plant because they are not equipped for this special job. Colonies of bumblebees were brought to Australia to pollinate the red clover. Now both thrive in that country.

An interesting partnership exists between the yucca plant and the yucca moth. Neither could live without the other. The moth gathers pollen from the stamens of a yucca flower and rolls it into a ball. Then it goes to the flower of another yucca plant, deposits its eggs in the ovary, and climbs up to the stigma where it places the pollen boll. This, of course, fertilizes the ovules and they grow into seeds. When the moth eggs are hatched, the larvae eat about one-third of the seeds. The others remain to produce more yucca plants. So the moth helps the yucca by carrying pollen to it, and the plant helps the moth by giving its young a home and food.

Insects, as we have seen, play a very important part in cross-pollination. But nature uses other methods too. She uses two other agents for special jobs. One of these agents is water which floats pollen to the tape grass plant, for instance. Another agent is the wind, upon which many trees, shrubs, and grasses depend for cross-pollination. Since the wind carries their pollen from the stamens to the pistils they do not have to be attractive, and so they do not have beautiful petals or fine fragrance. But wind is wasteful, and such plants must produce much more pollen than is actually needed.

In cross-pollination, nature sometimes resorts to special devices in order to make sure that a flower will not be pollinated by its own pollen. In the bloodroot, for instance, the pistil is ready to receive pollen before its own pollen is ripe. This means that bloodroot pistils have to depend upon insects to bring pollen from the stamens of another bloodroot flower. The case of the wild geranium is just the opposite of the bloodroot. Here the pollen is ready to be carried before its pistils are fully developed; and this flower, too, using the insect as a helper, is forced to depend upon cross-pollination for development of its seeds. Still a third way that nature has of making sure that only cross-pollination will take place is to give some flowers only stamens, and other flowers only pistils. A cottonwood tree is a good example of this.

After pollen grains have reached the pistil, they begin to take up moisture from the pistil. They swell and produce tiny tubes which grow through the pistil until they reach the ovules. When one of these pollen tubes reaches an ovule, some of its contents enter the ovule and unite with the egg cell inside. Then the egg cell begins to form a seed, and strange as it may seem, it is from this tiny seed that a whole new plant may grow.

L. Chace

The blossoms of the cottonwood tree

Black-Eyed Susan and Her Family

THE BLACK-EYED Susan belongs to the composite group of flowers. Like other composites it is made up of many little flowers, together on one head. Each "flower" is like a bouquet of flowers.

In fact, the black-eyed Susan is made up of two kinds of smaller flowers. All around the outside there is a row of bright yellow petals which hang down slightly. The flowers of this outer ring have neither stamens nor pistils and they serve only to attract insects. The many little, almost purple flowers on the inside or center have both stamens and pistils but no petals.

The stamens produce a bright yellow pollen, but the pistils of the same flower seldom are ready for it when its own pollen is ripe. The pollen is not wasted. It is carried by bees and other insects to black-eyed Susans ready for pollination.

In like manner the flower will obtain pollen at the time its pistils are ready to be pollinated. Often these flowers depend upon the wind to carry pollen to and from them.

Although the black-eyed Susan is often cultivated for its bright flowers, it is sometimes looked upon as a weed.

The sunflower, another composite, is often cultivated for its seeds. They are used as food for livestock and are valued for the oil they contain.

The composite is the largest family of flowering plants. Some are garden flowers like the daisy, chrysanthemum, zinnia, dahlia, and aster. Others grow wild like goldenrods, dandelions, ragweed, Spanish needle, Canada thistle, and the burdock.

Vegetable members of this large plant family are lettuce, endive, and artichoke.

The Lily Family

DID you know that the lovely white Easter Lily and the onion are members of the same family? Both belong to one of the largest of the plant families, the lily family.

People have been growing lilies for hundreds of years. There are several hundred different kinds of lilies. Some grow in hothouses and gardens. Other kinds of lilies grow wild in many sections of our country. The sego lily is the state flower of Utah. The yucca, another member of the lily family, is the state flower of New Mexico. The yucca is also called Spanish bayonet.

The plants in the lily family grow from scaly bulbs that send forth bare or leafy upright stems. The flowers usually have six petals and are bell-shaped. At the base of each petal is a groove that bears honey.

If you count the stamens in a lily flower, you will find that there are six. There is also a long pistil. Its tip is a three-lobed stigma.

While the flowers in the lily family are alike in certain ways, they may vary greatly in coloring. The Easter lily is white. The tiger lily is a brilliant orange-red. The hyacinth, also a member of this family, may be any of several colors.

Other well-known flowers in the lily family are the Madonna lily, the day lily, the wood lily, the tall leopard lily, and the fragrant lily of the valley.

The little dogtooth violet belongs to the lily family, too. Its flowers are gold-yellow and it grows in moist woods and swampy places beside brooks from Florida to Minnesota. The tulip is also a member of the lily family.

Like the onion, other members of the lily family are vegetables. Among these are asparagus, garlic, and the leek.

Philip Gendreau

The Rose Family

EACH TIME you bite into a juicy apple or eat a piece of cherry pie, you are tasting the fruit of a member of the rose family. The same is true of peaches, pears, and plums. Almost all fruit trees as well as strawberry and raspberry plants are relatives of the rosebush in your flower garden.

The members of the rose family have some parts of their flowers arranged in fives. There are usually five sepals which cover the bud. If inside the sepals there are more than five petals, they, too, are arranged in groups of fives. Sometimes it is hard to see this because the petals grow so close together. Inside the petals are several stamens and one or more pistils.

Let us see how a fruit grows from a blossom on a tree. Early in the spring a tall, healthy plum tree is bright with fragrant flowers. One of the blossoms may be especially beautiful, and bees visit it often to get its sweet nectar. They carry pollen from it and they, also, carry pollen to it from other flowers. Several pollen grains from other plum blossoms catch in the sticky top of the blossom's pistil. Usually, after pollination, a plum seed begins to grow and the petals of the blossom wilt and fall off.

On plum trees, the ovary of the blossom begins to grow as soon as the ovule inside is fertilized. The ovary part of the blossom, in time, becomes the fruit that we eat, and the ovule becomes the seed. As the seed grows, food for the young plant is stored in it.

Before long, the plum of this story becomes round and green, and during the summer it grows into a full-sized fruit. At last it turns a beautiful yellow with red on one side. It is now ready to eat.

160   If you plant the seed or pit of a plum, it should grow into a new

plum tree. But plum trees grow slowly and it usually takes several years for the little tree to become big enough to bear fruit. When the tree does begin to bear fruit, the fruit may be just like the plum from which the seed came. However, it might be very different because plum trees raised from seeds do not always produce fruit just like the plum from which the seed was produced.

New plants in the rose family often are not grown from seeds. To grow new rosebushes a branch from a choice plant is placed in the ground and new shoots or plants grow from the branch. New fruit trees usually are started from branches cut from fruit trees which have been selected because of their especially choice fruit. When people plant plum or other fruit trees, they want to be sure of the kind of fruit the tree will produce and they do not want to wait long enough for a tree to grow from a seed.

Rosebushes that are raised for their flowers also produce fruit. Many birds eat this fruit and often carry it with them as they fly, dropping the seeds. This is one of the reasons that rosebushes grow wild in many sections of the United States.

Four states—Iowa, North Dakota, Georgia, and New York—have chosen the rose as the state flower. Arkansas and Michigan have the apple blossom as the state flower; the peach blossom is the state flower of Delaware; and the hawthorne blossom is Missouri's state flower. These are all members of the rose family.

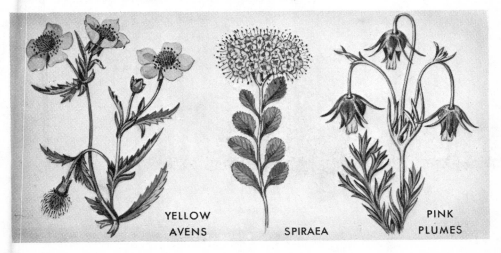

YELLOW AVENS SPIRAEA PINK PLUMES

These flowers belong to the rose family, too.

Oat   Wheat   Barley   Rye

Breakfast Grasses

HORSES, COWS, sheep, and many other animals eat grass. We, too, often eat grass, especially for breakfast. When we eat oatmeal, we are eating the seeds of oats, which is a grass. Corn flakes come from corn, another kind of grass. Cream of wheat, puffed rice, in fact, all our breakfast cereals, come from the grain of plants which are grasses.

Like the composite group, the grasses make up one of the largest plant families. All plants included in the grass family have flowers and stems which are much alike.

The flowers of grasses are not bright colored. They have no odor, and they have no petals. As grass flowers are pollinated by the wind, they do not need bright colored petals to attract insects. Since they do not need insects to help pollinate them, they do not produce

Rice   Corn

Thousands of years ago the people of Egypt made the first bread
and the people of China and India grew rice for food.

nectar and have no fragrance. Of course, insects do not bother to
visit grass flowers because they would get no nectar from them.

Corn is one of the most interesting kinds of grasses. This plant
produces two kinds of flowers, male flowers and female flowers. The
male flowers are borne on tassels. They grow on the very tops of the
corn plants and produce a great deal of pollen.

The female flowers are on the cobs, which grow along the sides
of the stems. There are many pistils on each cob and each pistil ends
in a threadlike fiber that protrudes from the top of the cob. Together,
all the fibers are called corn silk.

When the pollen on the tassel is ripe it may fall on the silk of the
same plant or it may be carried by the wind to another corn plant.
After pollen has reached the silk, it works its way down the long, fine
fiber of silk in order to reach an ovule and help make a seed, or
kernel.

Each of the hundreds of kernels on an ear of corn is the result of
pollen reaching a fiber of corn silk.

Corn grown from the seed of cross-pollinated plants is sometimes
stronger, healthier, and better able to stand bad weather. It may also
have larger and better shaped ears. Two carefully selected kinds of
corn are planted in alternate rows throughout the field. Just before
pollination, the tassels in all the rows containing one kind of corn
are clipped off. Then the silk of these corn plants cannot receive any

Before America was discovered the American Indians grew corn and the people of Japan, China, and India used bamboo for food and shelter.

pollen from the tassels of their own plants, but only the pollen which comes from the tassels of the other kind in the adjoining rows. In this way it is certain that half of the field, that is, the kind of corn from which the tassels have been removed, will be cross-pollinated. The corn which grows on these plants is called *hybrid* corn. Many farmers prefer to use only hybrid corn for seed.

The stems of corn plants each have a cradle-like path up one side. The outsides are exceptionally strong, and when the corn gets ripe in the fall, the stalks are very stiff and hard to break. The leaves are long and narrow, with tough veins running their full length. If the leaves were wider or did not have veins they would be torn more easily by the wind. Where the leaves are attached to the stems, they are fastened all the way around, as though they were wrapped. Although corn is bigger than other cereal plants, all are much alike in other ways. The stems of other grasses are also jointed, hard on the outside, and soft or hollow on the inside.

The cereal grasses—wheat, corn, oats, barley, rye, and rice—are man's chief sources of food. They also furnish food for the animals that supply our meat, milk, butter, cheese, and eggs.

Sugar cane and sorghum, which look much like corn, are also members of the grass family. Bamboo, another grass, probably has more different uses than any of the others. Bamboo is the largest of the grasses, growing sometimes to a height of nearly 100 feet.

A Vegetable Factory

HAVE you ever seen a vegetable factory? If there is a vegetable garden near your house, you can watch one in action. On a warm spring day, the gardener will spade up the vegetable plot, turning over the fresh black dirt on the surface. But he will be careful not to dig in the part of the garden where asparagus and rhubarb grow. These plants are *perennials,* and their roots live in the soil during the winter. The plants come up by themselves every spring.

In the freshly spaded part of the garden, the gardener will rake the surface dirt fine and smooth. Then he will mark out neat straight rows for radishes, lettuce, carrots, peas, and several other kinds of vegetables. Next he will rake in some fertilizer along the rows to make the dirt richer. Then he will plant the seeds according to the directions on each package.

Most of the seeds that will be planted will be those of *annuals,* plants which live only one year, produce seeds, and die. A few, like carrots, are really *biennials,* which the first year produce the large root that we eat, then wait until the next spring to come up again to produce seeds. But most people buy the seeds and plant these vegetables each year only for the food.

In one row, the gardener may plant onion sets which really are small onion bulbs, placing them about four inches apart to give them plenty of room to grow, and covering them with two inches of dirt.

The Parts We Eat

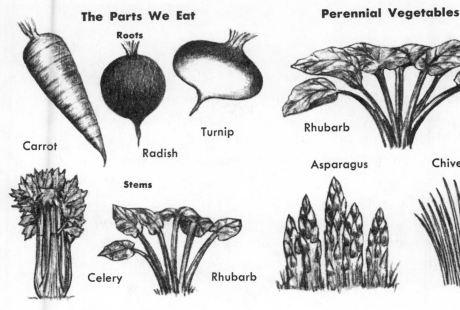

Roots

Carrot

Radish

Turnip

Stems

Celery

Rhubarb

Perennial Vegetables

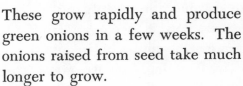

Rhubarb

Asparagus

Chives

Stalks and Flowers

Broccoli

Cauliflower

Seeds

Beans

Corn

Fruit

Pumpkin

Tomato

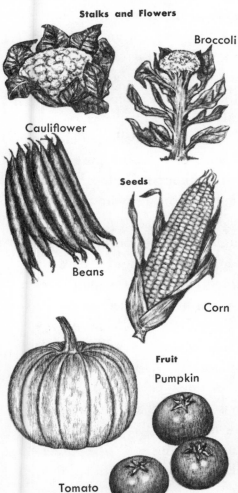

These grow rapidly and produce green onions in a few weeks. The onions raised from seed take much longer to grow.

On the first planting day, the gardener will be careful to plant only vegetables which can stand cold weather. About a month later, when the danger of frost is past, he will plant beans and corn and also may set out tomato, cabbage, and cauliflower plants which he has grown from seeds in a warm, sunny place indoors or which he may secure from a seed store. When plants are moved this way, it is called *transplanting*. It enables the gardener to have big plants in a garden early in the season.

The gardener will set out some of these plants between the rows of seeds which have been planted earlier. Some of the other vegetables, such as radishes, will be

167

ready to eat early. They will be gone by the time the vegetables that have been planted later will need more room to grow.

If the gardener finds he has enough ground left, he may decide to plant a few hills of potatoes. He will use good, medium-sized potatoes for seeds, cutting them apart so that each piece has one *eye*. The eye of a potato is really a bud. The buds grow fast. Soon a potato plant will be growing from almost every eye.

Why do we call a vegetable garden a vegetable factory? These vegetables provide an important part of the food we eat. These vegetables also make, or manufacture, the food which they store in the parts we eat.

We eat different parts of different kinds of vegetables. The main food value of a green garden plant may be in the roots, stems, buds, leaves, flowers, seeds, or fruits. We eat the roots of radishes and carrots, the bulbs of onions, the stems and leafstalks of celery, the stems and buds of asparagus, the leaves of lettuce, the flowers of cauliflower, the seeds and sometimes the pods of beans and peas, and the fruit of the tomato.

Each part of a plant is made of millions of tiny cells which are fitted together like tiny rooms. Each part serves a purpose. For example, the root cells absorb water and minerals from the soil. But the most wonderful process, the manufacture of sugar for plant growth, takes place in the cells of the green leaves.

The leaves contain tiny openings through which carbon dioxide gas from the air enters. Water enters through the roots and comes up through the stems. A green substance called *chlorophyll*, which gives the leaves their color, is in the cells. Sugar is produced from the carbon dioxide and water by action of the chlorophyll. The energy for this work is furnished by sunlight. This process by which plants manufacture their food is called *photosynthesis*. Without photosynthesis, there would be no food for plants or animals.

After sugar is formed in the leaves, most plants change some of it to another kind of food before they store it away. The potato plant changes much of the sugar to starch before storing it in the underground stem. Peas and beans form proteins from much of their sugar, and, as they do so, they store the proteins in the seeds.

Balsam
Fir

Hemlock

White
Pine

White
Spruce

Loblolly
Pine

Our Christmas Tree

MANY boys and girls look at the bright ornaments and lights on their Christmas tree without knowing what kind of tree it is. The trees most often used for Christmas are spruce, balsam fir, and Douglas fir. Pine, cedar, or hemlock are also used sometimes.

These and other trees that have green leaves throughout the year are called *evergreens*. They do not keep the same leaves year after year. Their change of leaves usually goes unnoticed because the old leaves are not shed until new ones are formed. This way of changing leaves makes these trees appear green year after year, summer, winter, spring, and fall.

They are different from trees such as the maple which shed all their leaves in the fall. Those trees are called *deciduous* trees.

You can tell the different evergreens by their branches.

Spruce

Balsam Fir

Douglas Fir

Pine

Hemlock

Cedar

The kinds of evergreens that usually are used as Christmas trees bear cones and have slender, needle-like leaves. The cones and needles on the different kinds are not at all alike. It is easy to tell most of them apart by their needles.

Spruce needles are four sided, sharp pointed, and about three-quarters of an inch in length. The needles of fir trees are also short, but they are flat and blunt, arranged in rows on opposite sides of the branches. Leaves of the balsam fir are quite broad at the place where they are attached to the twigs. Those of the Douglas fir are narrow at the place where they are attached to the twigs.

While the spruce makes one of the loveliest Christmas trees, some people do not like to use it because its needles are very sharp. The needles grow thickly around the branches, pointing in all directions, and may prick you when you come near.

The balsam fir is a popular Christmas tree because it does not shed its needles as quickly as the other evergreens do after they are cut down.

These giant redwood trees of California are one of nature's wonders. For many years they were chopped down in great quantities for lumber. The great naturalist John Muir fought to preserve these trees and today there are laws to regulate their cutting. In 1908 the United States acquired a huge tract of redwoods and created a national monument, Muir Woods, a few miles from San Francisco.

Pine trees are not used often as Christmas trees because a sticky pitch oozes from the bark of most pines. Pine needles are usually two inches or more long and two or more needles grow together in a cluster or bundle. Hemlock needles are usually less than half an inch long. They are flat and blunt with a much lighter green color underneath than on top. The leaves of cedar trees are not needle-like but instead are either awl-shaped or flat.

Like flowers, the cones of these evergreen trees become pollinated and produce seeds. As an example of how these seeds are formed, let us follow the story of a white pine tree's seeds.

Early in the spring, short reddish brown tufts, or *catkins*, appear near the tips of some of the twigs of the tree. There are several of these catkins in each cluster and they produce pollen. On the tips, or near the tips, of many other branches tiny pinkish-green cones appear. They point up in the air and, like the pistils of flowers, receive the pollen. The cones are made up of many scales, and at the base of each scale there are two ovules.

During the warm spring days the pollen ripens and is picked up by the wind. It is carried easily because each little grain has two wings. In the meantime, the cones open and spread their scales like many little shovels. So much pollen from the catkins is given off into the air that some of it is sure to be carried down behind the many little scales of the cones. After the cones are pollinated, the scales close back against the cones; then the cones slowly turn and point downward.

Closed cone

Catkin drops
pollen on cone.

Open cone
drops seeds.

After the pollen grains close in behind the scales, the pollen tubes grow into the ovules. Two seeds begin to form behind each scale. When the pine cone is about two years old, the scales open and the seeds fall out. Each little winged seed is carried away by the wind. Some seeds reach fertile soil and grow into new pine trees.

When the early settlers came to North America, there were many forests of pine, cedar, spruce, and other trees. Today much of this forest land is gone, cut down for timber and to provide soil for food crops. Now we are trying to conserve our forests, for we know that they are an important natural resource. Trees provide us with lumber and paper. They also act as windbreaks and help keep top soil from being carried away by heavy rains. We still cut down trees—but we also plant new trees.

We plant Christmas tree farms, too, to preserve our evergreens. The trees are planted in rows and are cut down when they are between three and five years old. This leaves more room for the other trees to grow. It also allows the Christmas tree farmer to sell part of his tree crop each year and still keep a fine grove of trees.

Do you know that Christmas trees are decorated in different ways in countries around the world? The Swiss tree wears snow and pine cones and gilded nuts. The Dutch tree has paper shoes of many colors. The Japanese tree is trimmed with tangerines and rice fortune cookies. Do you like the way this Polish Christmas tree is decorated?

Giants of the Forest

A LARGE house may be thirty feet high and a large shade tree may be twice as high. But some of the sequoia trees in California are more than 300 feet tall or five times as tall as most large shade trees. Some of them are more than thirty feet across at the base. They were named for Sequoyah, a famous Indian, the one who invented the Cherokee alphabet.

There are two kinds of these trees, the giant sequoias, or "big trees", and the redwoods. The redwoods are the taller of the two kinds but the "big trees" are larger around. Some of the giant sequoias now standing are more than 3,000 years old. They were old trees when Columbus discovered America, and many of them were living long before the time that Christ was born.

The redwoods get their name from the deep reddish color of their wood. They are native only along the foggy coastal regions of northern California and Oregon, while the giant sequoias grow inland in central California on the western slopes of the Sierra Nevadas. Both kinds of sequoias are evergreens and bear cones. The redwoods are ready to shed their seeds in a year, but it takes two years for the cone of the "big trees" to become ripe.

A Giant Sequoia

There are no large forests of sequoias left. When people began to settle in California the trees were cut down to make way for homes and farms. Years later people began to be concerned about what was happening to their forests. Concern led to an action to save them. Now the best sequoia groves are protected by the United States Government as a part of our National Forests.

174

PLANTS WITHOUT SEEDS

Giant Plants of the Sea

THE biggest plants in all the oceans of the world are the giant kelps. These huge plants sometimes grow to a length of 150 feet. They do not stand up straight and tall like trees. They look more like vines.

These strange plants do not have roots like land plants. Instead they have *holdfasts* which anchor the plants to the shallow bottom of the ocean along rocky shores.

Giant kelps do not have real leaves either. They do, however, have organs that look something like leaves that may be a yard long and ten inches wide. A small air bladder at the base of each leaf-like organ acts as a float and helps keep parts of the kelp near the top of the water where they can get sunlight. Like other green plants, kelps need light with which to manufacture the food they need.

These plants are perennials and live many years. New plants grow from the holdfasts. Kelp plants reproduce by means of spores instead of seeds.

This kelp was washed ashore by the waves along a California beach. Like many other kinds of ocean plants, giant kelp is often called seaweed. Seaweed is used in many different ways. Some people eat it, some use it as a fertilizer, and some feed it to their animals. We also get many useful things from seaweed. One of them, called agar, is used to make such products as candy and sherbet.

Fiddle Heads

Fiddleheads, Fronds, and Ferns

URING the Coal Age, many thousands of years ago, there were immense forests of ferns that grew as tall as our trees do now. Compared with those ancient plants, the ferns that we know today seem very tiny. We often use them for house plants or as green leaves in bouquets of flowers.

When ferns first come through the ground, each leafy branch, or frond, is rolled up into a ball which unrolls as it grows. When partly open the frond is shaped so much like the head of a violin that young ferns are often called "fiddle heads". This is a good way to tell whether a plant is a fern or not, because all true ferns have fiddle heads and they are the only plants that do.

Ferns have no flowers or seeds. Instead many ferns have little cases that look like small brown dots on the under side of the leaves. These cases contain many tiny spores. Although a fern spore has but one cell and is so small that it can be seen only under a microscope, it serves the fern much as a seed does a seed plant. When the spore cases are ripe, they spring open with enough force to throw the spores into the air. The wind carries them and those that fall in places where the soil and temperature are right and where there is plenty of moisture live and grow.

A Coal Age forest looked like this.

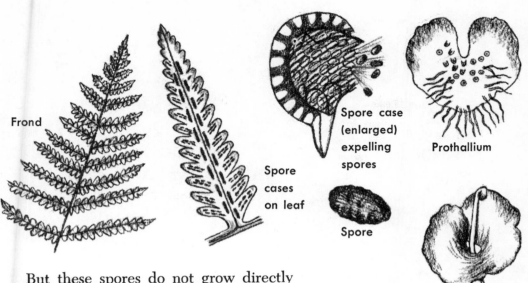

Frond

Spore cases on leaf

Spore case (enlarged) expelling spores

Spore

Prothallium

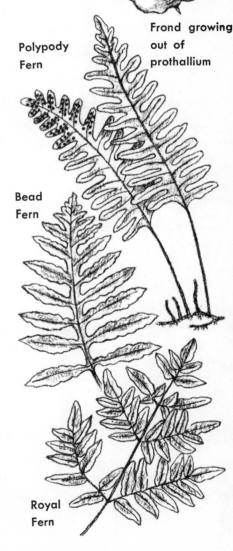

Polypody Fern

Frond growing out of prothallium

Bead Fern

Royal Fern

But these spores do not grow directly into ferns, as you might expect. Instead, each grows into a little flat green body no bigger than your thumb nail and shaped somewhat like a heart. It clings to the ground by hairlike roots. This little plant body is called a *prothallium,* which means "before the shoot". Two types of bumps grow on the under side of the prothallium. Although these small bumps do not have stamens and pistils, they do for the pro-thallium what stamens and pistils do for flowers. When the bumps are ripe, the male cells of the one type travel forth, in moisture, in all directions. When one of these cells reaches the second kind of bump it unites with a female cell of that particular bump and a real fern begins to grow. The new plant grows slowly. After several years it may develop into a full-sized fern.

Ferns usually grow in deep woods where it is shady and moist. There are many different kinds of ferns. Some of the most beautiful are the lacy Maidenhair, the Royal Fern, and the Bead Fern.

Parasol Plants
and Their Relatives

THE PLANTS that we have learned about so far, the flowers, trees, ferns, and seaweeds, all are alike in one very important way. All of them have the green coloring matter called chlorophyll. By means of this chorophyll they are able to make their own food.

We come now to very different kinds of plants, those that are not green. And because they have none of the green chlorophyll, they cannot make food for themselves, but have to depend on other plants for food. That is, they use or steal food that has been made by plants that are green. Such a plant is a *fungus* and when we speak of more than one of them, they are called *fungi*.

Among the largest and most interesting of these fungi are the mushrooms, of which there are many kinds. Some live on the trunks or limbs of trees, taking from the trees food which their green leaves have manufactured. Those that grow on the ground live on the decayed material from dead green plants, and thus use food which was stored up by these plants when they were living.

Like ferns and kelps, mushrooms have tiny spores instead of seeds. Sometimes we are able to shake a fine dust from a mushroom. This dust is really millions of tiny spores. Few of the mushroom spores live because only a few of them land in suitable places. They grow best in warm, moist places and most kinds need shade.

Let us see what may happen when one of these little spores from a parasol mushroom plant is carried by the wind to some rich, moist soil. It is not in the soil long before it takes in a great deal of water and begins to swell. By and by a fine white thread begins to grow from the side. The little thread takes food from decaying plants. It grows fast, branching again and again until a network of rootlike threads has formed. This network of threads is called the *mycelium*.

Then a tiny little knob or button begins to grow on the side of one of the threads. It grows to be as large as the end of your little finger.

One day the weather becomes very warm and the button grows so fast that it pushes through the top of the ground. The button breaks around the top of the stem and the cap is raised. It is no longer a button mushroom but a raised white parasol. It keeps on growing until its parasol cap is perhaps five inches wide and its handle, or stem, may be nine inches long.

Under the cap of the mushroom there are many folds which hang down like white curtains, one close to another. These are called gills and tiny white spores grow on the sides of them. When the spores are ripe some of them are dropped on the ground and others may be carried far away by the wind.

After the spores ripen and leave, the parasol part of the plant dies, but the threadlike roots under the ground continue to live. New little bumps are formed and the first warm, moist day other mushrooms are almost sure to appear.

Many mushrooms are shaped like umbrellas. Most of them have gills and form spores in the same way, but not all of the spores are white like those of the parasol mushroom. The orange-milk mushroom has yellowish brown spores, the meadow mushroom has pink ones, while the inky-cap has black spores. These four kinds of mushrooms are edible, but many kinds are not.

Oyster mushrooms have gills and white spores but are not shaped like umbrellas. They grow so close to one another that they look like one oyster on top of another. Often they have no stems, but grow fast to trees. If they have stems they are fastened at one side of the cap instead of in the middle. These mushrooms, too, are good to eat.

A morel mushroom is especially prized for food. It has a cap shaped somewhat like a sponge. It has no gills and the spores grow in tiny sacs in the cap. This mushroom usually grows three or four inches tall.

One of the most beautiful kinds is the sulphur mushroom which grows on the trunks of trees. Sometimes it is called a shelf fungus because it looks much like a shelf. It does not have gills or sacs but little pores in which the spores grow. This mushroom is a bright yellow color, like sulphur, from which it gets its name.

Oyster Mushroom   Shaggy Cap   Parasol   Puff Ball   Earth Star

A tree with sulphur mushrooms growing on it is almost sure to die because the threadlike "roots" steal so much of its food. The mushrooms which grow on trees, also, may endanger the trees because the threads open up the bark so that insects may attack them easily.

Another kind of mushroom, often found growing in pastures, is called a puff ball. Sometimes these grow larger than basketballs while others may be as small as marbles. If these mushrooms are gathered at the right time they are good to eat. When ripe they are almost full of dust, which is really millions of spores.

The earth star mushroom is shaped like a star. Like the puff ball, it is almost full of spores when it is ripe. They come out through a little hole at the top of the plant. Most earth stars are not more than two or three inches across when the points are stretched out flat. The earth star is sometimes called "the poor man's weather glass" because the points curl back or down when the weather is dry, but when the weather is wet the points straighten out again.

Many mushrooms are helpful to people because they furnish nourishing food which is easy to prepare. Some also help dead leaves and twigs decay to make rich soil.

But mushrooms NEVER should be gathered to eat except by someone who knows a great deal about mushrooms because certain kinds are very poisonous. Unfortunately the poisonous kinds, which some people call "toadstools", look very much like some of the harmless ones. One of the most beautiful mushrooms—the amanita—if eaten, is more deadly than a rattle snake bite.

Sulphur Shelf   Fairy Ring   Morel   Inky Cap

A Mold Garden

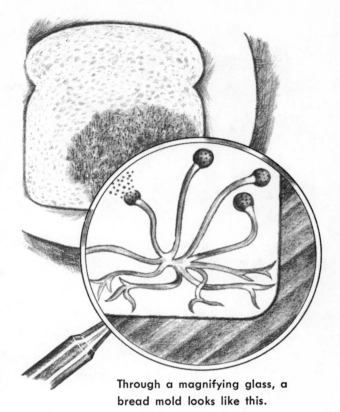

Through a magnifying glass, a bread mold looks like this.

THERE IS a kind of garden that you can make very easily. In fact, you may have made one without meaning to if you have happened to leave any moist food in a warm dark place for a few days. It soon becomes covered with mold, which is a growth of many little plants.

Mold plants are dependent because they cannot make their own food. They must use for food that which has been manufactured by plants with green leaves. Mold plants are able to live and grow on almost anything which comes from plants and animals.

To make a mold garden you do not need soil, or sunshine, and not much water. Simply take a dish and put in it some pieces of bread, orange, or almost any food which you have. Unless it is quite moist, sprinkle it with water, as mold needs moisture to grow. It is a good plan to cover the dish because the cover keeps the food moist. Then set it in a warm place out of the sunlight.

You need not be concerned about planting your mold garden, it already has been planted. Although you did not see that planting it has happened just the same. Like mushrooms, mold plants are fungi and grow from tiny spores. The air contains many mold spores all the time. Of course many of them never have a chance to grow because they do not find suitable places.

A little spore which reaches a suitable growing place soon begins to get bigger and sends out little white threads. The white threads branch and soon there is a network of them growing on and into the food. Like the root-like threads of a mushroom, this body of threads

These four kinds of slime molds are shown highly magnified as seen under a microscope.

is called a mycelium. Each thread of a mold plant is so tiny that you can see it only with a microscope.

When the mold plants are ready to produce spores, they send up stems that are so tiny that many of them, together, look like a covering of beautifully colored fur. The spores are produced on or near the ends of these threads.

Some kinds of mold produce spores in small round cases at the ends of the stems. The spore cases may be colored—black, blue, green, or yellow. You may find all or only part of the colors in your mold garden.

There are many kinds of mold and not all of them would grow in a dish of bread or oranges. Molds grow on almost everything which comes from plants and animals. They grow on leather and cloth as well as food.

Some kinds of mold are used to help make food for us. Several kinds of cheese get their special flavors because of the mold which has been planted in them. If you have tasted creamy white cheese with bluish streaks through it, you may be sure the streaks were mold. A certain kind of blue mold has become famous because of its importance in making a drug called penicillin.

There is a class of molds called slime molds that are valuable because they cause old dead plants to decay and make the soil richer. Sometime when you are in the woods, you may pull the loose bark from an old log and find patches of bright colors—red, blue, yellow, or brown. These probably are the spores of a kind of slime mold.

Like mushrooms, molds may be our friends or our enemies. But since we know that they do not grow and flourish in moving air, or in places that are light, dry or cold, we, therefore, can keep them from growing in places where we do not want them, and can help them to grow where we do want them.

The Plant that Eats Sugar

LONG AGO people ate bread that was solid all the way through. They did not know how to make any other kind. Then it was found that dough a day or two old would puff up when it was left standing in a warm place. Bread baked from this dough was full of little holes and much easier to eat. But people did not understand what made the dough puff up.

If the microscope had not been invented, we might still be wondering what makes some bread light and fluffy. We, also, might be wondering what makes good sweet fruit juice ferment and become sour and bitter. Now we know that tiny yeast plants are the magicians that do these tricks. The air always contains many yeast spores.

Yeast plants have only one cell and depend on sugar for their food. If the temperature is warm and there is sugar and water, yeast plants grow and produce more plants like themselves very rapidly. Little bumps which are really buds or baby plants grow out on the sides of the older plants. As the buds get larger, they too, may form buds of their own. Sometimes the buds hang together like a string of beads. Usually, however, they fall apart and start new strings.

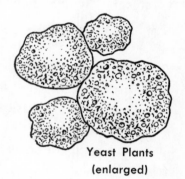

Yeast Plants
(enlarged)

Like all other living things, yeast plants not only use food as they grow, but they throw off materials which are useless to them. While the yeast plants use sugar as food they throw off carbon dioxide gas and alcohol. Carbon dioxide is the gas which green plants use when they make food, but as yeast plants do not make their own food, they have no use for it.

Bread dough is almost all flour, water, sugar, and salt. It is very thick and tough and will stretch if it is pulled. The carbon dioxide given off by the yeast plants cannot get through the dough. The dough stretches and this makes room for the gas. Soon there are little pockets of gas all through the dough. The dough takes up much

more space than it did, and we say the dough "rises." When the bread is baked, the yeast is killed. The alcohol evaporates and the carbon dioxide gas escapes, leaving the bread full of little holes where the gas once was.

Nowadays instead of making bread from old dough into which yeast plants have made their way, most people make fresh dough and add yeast cakes which they can buy. The cakes contain millions of tiny yeast plants, but these plants are prevented from growing in the cake due to a lack of enough food or moisture. Refrigeration, too, prevents their growth so yeast cakes usually are kept in cool and dry places.

Yeast plants, also, get into fruit juices when the juices stand in open air. They cause the fruit juices to lose their sweetness by using up the sugar as they grow in it. The carbon dioxide gas that is given off comes up in bubbles through the liquid, but the alcohol remains. It is in this way that wine and other alcoholic drinks are made. One reason for canning food is to keep it from fermenting. The food that is to be canned is first heated to kill the yeast and other plants such as molds and bacteria. Then it is sealed in the cans to prevent the air from getting to it.

Although yeast plants have only one cell and are so tiny they can be seen only through a microscope, they are very important to us. They are very useful because they make bread rise and make alcohol. They can be mischief-makers when they cause fruit juices to ferment when we want to keep them sweet, but as we have seen, there are ways of preventing such fermentation.

The World's Tiniest Plants

THE SMALLEST plant that we know about is a bacterium. When we speak of more than one of these plants, the word used is "bacteria." Like a yeast plant, but much smaller, a bacterium has only one cell in its whole body. Some kinds of bacteria are smaller than others, but all are so tiny that it would take thousands of them to cover the period at the end of this sentence.

Until the microscope was invented in the 1600's, people did not know that bacteria existed. The man who probably was the first to see bacteria called them "little beasties" because he thought that they were animals.

Bacteria can make more plants like themselves faster than any other known plant. In some cases it takes only twenty minutes for a single bacterium to grow into two bacteria.

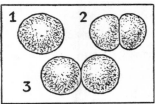

How Bacteria Multiply

A bacterium takes in food and water, and soon a double wall grows through the center of the cell. The double wall then divides, leaving two cells instead of one. Each of the new cells may divide in the same way in another twenty minutes. By the end of four hours, multiplying at this rate and if all of them live, there would be over 4,000 bacteria instead of one tiny bacterium.

If you were to look through a microscope at some bacteria you might see round ones, rod-shaped ones, or curly ones. There are many kinds of bacteria but they usually are shaped in one of these three ways.

Bacteria are found almost everywhere in

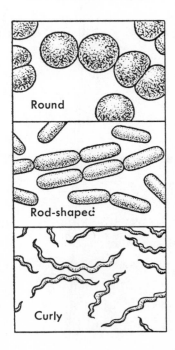

Round

Rod-shaped

Curly

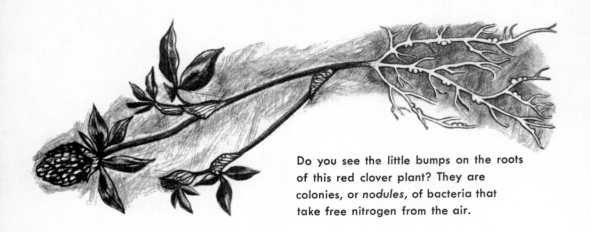

Do you see the little bumps on the roots of this red clover plant? They are colonies, or *nodules,* of bacteria that take free nitrogen from the air.

the world—in the air, in water, in the soil, on our hands, and even in our bodies. Many kinds are helpful to animals and plants; others are the cause of some of our worst diseases.

First let us see what the helpful bacteria may do. They cause the decay of dead plants and animals. If they could not do this important work, the earth soon would be piled high with dead things. When bacteria decay waste materials, valuable substances are returned to the soil to enrich it.

Some bacteria help us to make certain kinds of food such as cheese and butter. Bacteria help to digest some of our food in our bodies.

A helpful kind, called nitrogen-fixing bacteria, lives in little bumps on the roots of certain plants such as clover. As they grow, these bacteria take nitrogen gas from the air and put it into the soil in a form which the plant can use. Green plants need nitrogen compounds in order to grow, and they can get them only from the soil.

The harmful bacteria, often called germs or microbes, are not very likely to harm us if we eat clean food and keep our bodies clean and healthy. We know enough about bacteria now so that we are able to protect ourselves against most of them.

For example, we know that by keeping food cool in refrigerators, bacteria cannot grow well in it. If food is heated most of the bacteria are killed, and then by sealing it so that no more of these plants can get in, the food can be kept clean and sweet for long periods. Also, drying some foods has been found to be a good way of preserving them, since most bacteria cannot grow where it is dry.

All in all, these tiny plants are much more helpful than harmful, and we would have a very queer world without them.

How Plants and Animals Help Each Other

ALL THE STORIES in this book have been about either plants or animals. Yet as you look around, you will see that where there are plants, there are usually animals, too. There is a simple reason for this. Plants and animals depend upon each other.

Most green plants can make their own food, for all they need is sunlight, air, water, and soil that is filled with minerals.

Other living things, even meat-eating animals, eat food that comes directly or indirectly from green plants. For example, we eat beef. Beef comes from a cow. The cow eats grass. These steps, or links, make up what is called a *food chain*. Without green plants, all other living things would in time die of starvation.

Plants also help animals by providing them with homes and shelter. Many birds build their nests in trees. Deer and other animals use brush for shelter. Beavers cut down trees to build their lodges. Even man depends upon plants for shelter because trees furnish lumber for houses.

In this food chain, the little fishes are eating
small plants. The larger fishes eat the small fishes.
The boy will catch and eat the large fish.

How do animals help plants? You have read how bees and other insects and some birds pollinate plants. Animals also help some plants by scattering their seeds. In these ways, animals help plants spread and grow.

Even after they are dead, plants and animals help each other. When leaves fall and flowers die, they decay. Animals decay, too, when they die. Rain and snow help this decayed matter sink into the soil. This enriches the soil by adding chemicals to it. From the soil, green plants grow and animals eat them and so the food circle, or *cycle*, continues.

Plants and animals help each other in another important way. Each gives off waste matter the other can use. When they breathe, animals take oxygen from the air and give off carbon dioxide. Plants take the carbon dioxide from the air and use it in making food. They return oxygen to the air. Animals breathe in the oxygen. Again you can see the cycle in action. Plants and animals help each other to survive.

In the tropical jungles and
on the arctic snows,
on land and sea and in the air,
the cycle of life goes on.
Plants and animals depend upon
each other for survival.

Because plants and animals depend upon each other in many ways, nature keeps a balance between them. Usually there will be about as many plants as there are animals. Here are some of the ways this natural balance works.

Each year some baby plants and animals die because they are too weak to live. Diseases also kill some plants and animals. The strong and hardy survive.

Then, too, all plants and animals have their enemies. Insects eat plants, and birds eat insects. Other animals kill birds. The cycle goes on and on.

Weather also helps keep the balance between plants and animals. For example, if there is too much rain it can wash away soil and some of the plants that grow in it. If there is too little rain, some plants will die because they need water to grow.

If the number of plants in a place decreases, some animals will die. Others will leave to find new places where plants grow more plentifully. The plants that survive and the animals that survive and stay in that place will balance each other.

As long as living things depend upon each other, nature keeps a balance between them.

INDEX